MEL BAY'S COMPLETE JAZZ SAX BOOK

By William Bay

Contents

SECTION ONE:
Jazz Sax Studies

Phrase #1

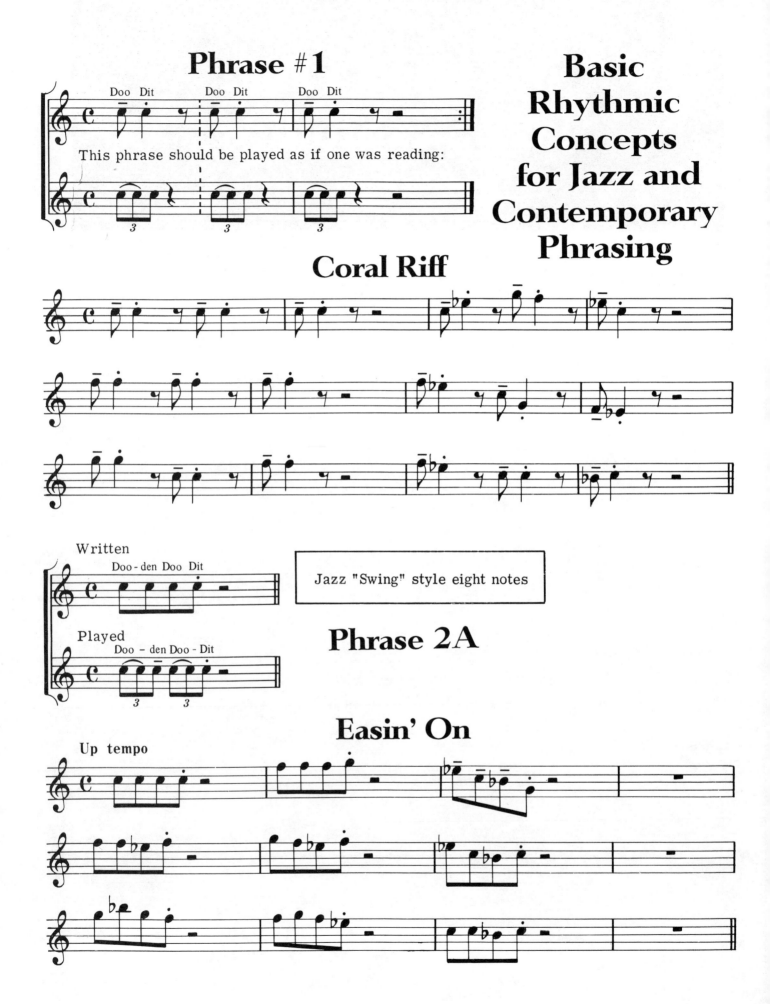

Coral Riff

Jazz "Swing" style eight notes

Phrase 2A

Easin' On

4

Phrase #2B

Jazz Study

Easy Feelin'

Mixed Bag

M.J.

Go!

Phrase #3A

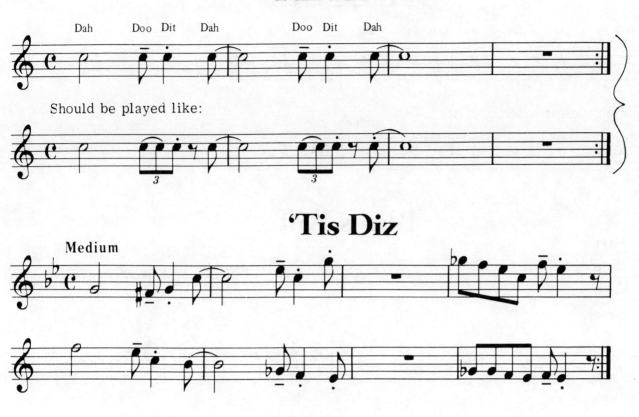

'Tis Diz

Phrase #3B

Flyin' High

Phase #4

This phrase can also be written:

Blues Riff

Phrase #5

Keep' em Short

Phrase #6

The "DOT" sound is a heavy accent, while the "DIT" is short, but not meant to be heavily accented.

Easy Groovin'

Phrase #7

Smooth legato tonguing is essential for much of jazz music.
Give all notes full value, separate them with very light tonguing, and keep them "Swinging."

"Smooth-Doo-Tonguing"

9

Phrase #8 "Slow-Doo-Dot"

Starlight Sounds

Phrase #9 "Swing Riff"

Freddie's Jump

Phrase #10

Big Band Bash

10

Phrase #11

Opus 11

Phrase #12

Jersey Stomp

11

Phrase #12

Soft Winds

Phrase #13

Happy Swing

Phrase #14

"3/4 Jazz"

Walkin'

Phrase #15

"Doo-Dot-Doo-Dot"

Revival Blues

Bossa Nova Style

In this style, and all othes latin styles, the eighth notes are played "Straight", and not in the "Swing" style.

"To Carlos"

Latin Holiday

Basic Style
Easy Blowin'

Whose Blues

Special Effects

The Standardization of Stage Band Articulations

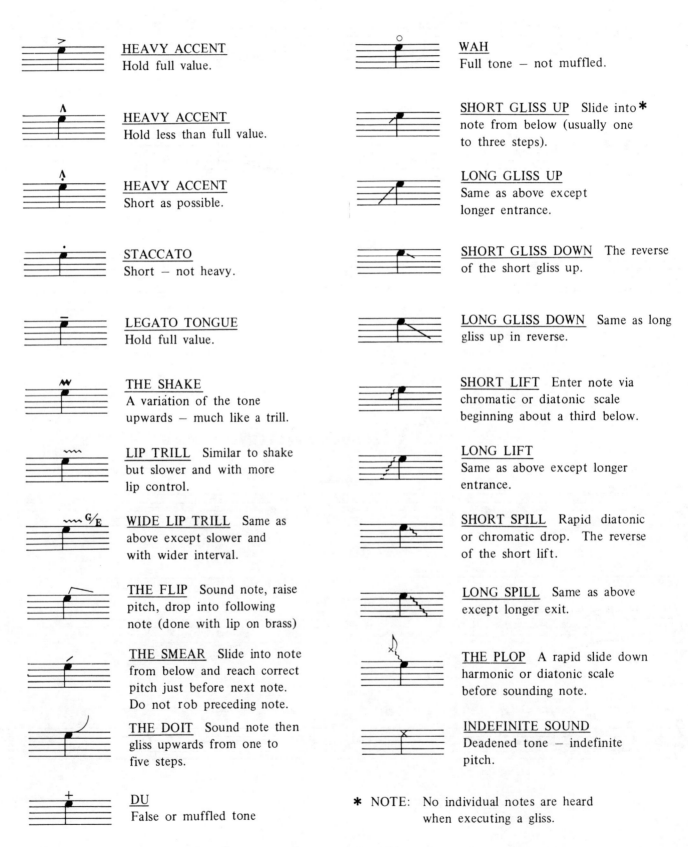

HEAVY ACCENT
Hold full value.

HEAVY ACCENT
Hold less than full value.

HEAVY ACCENT
Short as possible.

STACCATO
Short — not heavy.

LEGATO TONGUE
Hold full value.

THE SHAKE
A variation of the tone
upwards — much like a trill.

LIP TRILL Similar to shake
but slower and with more
lip control.

WIDE LIP TRILL Same as
above except slower and
with wider interval.

THE FLIP Sound note, raise
pitch, drop into following
note (done with lip on brass)

THE SMEAR Slide into note
from below and reach correct
pitch just before next note.
Do not rob preceding note.

THE DOIT Sound note then
gliss upwards from one to
five steps.

DU
False or muffled tone

WAH
Full tone — not muffled.

SHORT GLISS UP Slide into *
note from below (usually one
to three steps).

LONG GLISS UP
Same as above except
longer entrance.

SHORT GLISS DOWN The reverse
of the short gliss up.

LONG GLISS DOWN Same as long
gliss up in reverse.

SHORT LIFT Enter note via
chromatic or diatonic scale
beginning about a third below.

LONG LIFT
Same as above except longer
entrance.

SHORT SPILL Rapid diatonic
or chromatic drop. The reverse
of the short lift.

LONG SPILL Same as above
except longer exit.

THE PLOP A rapid slide down
harmonic or diatonic scale
before sounding note.

INDEFINITE SOUND
Deadened tone — indefinite
pitch.

* NOTE: No individual notes are heard
when executing a gliss.

Used by permission from the National Association of Jazz Educators

16

Articulations
Heavy Accent #1
(Hold Full Value)

Heavy Accent #2
(Hold Less Than Full Value)

Heavy Accent #3
(Short as Possible)

Standard Staccato

In jazz and contemporary music, the staccato note is played short, but lightly, and not with a heavy tongue.

Standard Legato
(Hold Full Value, Use Light Tongue)

The Shake

Like a trill; usually done by trilling a minor third (three half steps) from the written note.

would be played as

The Flip

A type of "turn" involving notes abore and below the written note.

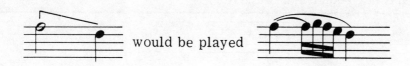

would be played

The Smear

Sounding a note below pitch, then slowly bringing it up to pitch just before the next note. This is done by relaxing the embouchure and slightly dropping the jaw to flatten the note, and then bringing the note up to pitch close to the end of its duration. The smear may also be achieved by half-closing the key one-half step below the written note, while also fingering the actual note.

This techique is also called "bending", and is some times notated as:

19

The Doit

Sound the written note, then "Slide" up one to five steps. The notes in the "Slide"(or gliss) should not sound individually.

Short Up Gliss

"Sliding" into a note from one to three steps below its written pitch. This can be done with the embouchure and jaw with or without fingering the gliss notes.

Long Up Gliss

Same as short gliss up, but from a greater distance below the written note. Fingering the notes would be neccessary. Start three steps to an octave below the written note.

In both cases the actual pitch should be reached at the time that the note would be played if there was no gliss. In other words, the gliss must be played "before the beat".

Gliss Study

Short Down Gliss

Also called short fall-off. Play the written note for about one-half of its value, them quickly "Slide" down chromatically.
The chromatic notes should not sound individually, and there should not be any particular pitch in evidence at the end of the gliss!

Long Down Gliss

Also called long fall-off. Similar to short gliss down except that the written note is held a little longer and the gliss goes lower and slower.

Basie style blues

Connecting Gliss

A gliss between two notes. If the notes are no more than a third (two steps) apart, use the chromatic scale to connect them. If the notes are more than a third apart, use an applicable major or minor scale.Let the first note sound for at least half of its value before starting the gliss.

Short Lift

Start about three steps below the written note and "rip" into it using chromatic and/or diatonic movement.

Long Lift

Start about five or six steps below and use diatonic movement to "rip" into the note.

Lifts

Spills

The reverse of the lift;keys should be heard moving after the air has stopped.

Short Spill   ### Long Spill

Spill Spell

Plop

A type of spill, done from about a fifth above the written note. The scale is played very quickly and clarity of scale notes is not important.

Plopping Along

Indefinite Sound

Also called "ghosting". The note is played with a deadened tone, and is "inferred" rather than actually played out. The effect is produced by laying the top of the tongue against the reed, which mutes the tone. Do not press hard against the reed as this can close off the mouthpiece completely.

Indefinitely

Be-Bop

Much of today's jazz remains under the influence of "be-bop" phrasing. All of the following studies should be played slowly at first. Keep the tonguing light. Remember- the studies should swing. They should not sound mechanical. Use breath accents for phrasing instead of a lot of tonguing.

Changes

Riff for Clifford

25

Breezin'

Be-Bop Blue

Medium groove

Theme for Bird

26

The Messenger

Cookin'

Up tempo

Cool Affair

Rock

Rock music is characterised by hard-driving "even-eights" rhythms. The swing-style eighth note approach is not used in rock.

Study #1

Rhythm Exercise

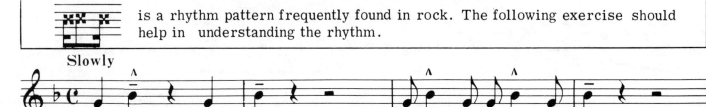

is a rhythm pattern frequently found in rock. The following exercise should help in understanding the rhythm.

Slowly

Study #2

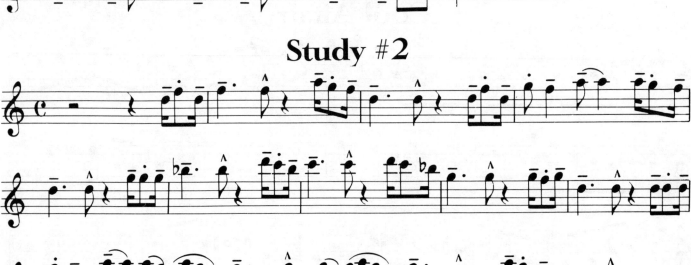

Study #3

Soul Riff

Soul Groove

Detroit Dance

Choctaw Bridge

Aretha

Midnight Ride

Hard Driver

Blues Riff

Soul Prelude

Rhythm

Motown Groove

Basically Soul

Chicago

Latin Rock

West Side Slide

Blues Boogie

Blues Bop

In a be-bop style blues like this, almost no tongue is used, and most phrasing is achieved by the use of breath accents.

Jazz Techniques

Jazz and Contemporary Music requires certain techniques (especially in solo performance) which frequently are not perfected in studying traditional saxophone literature. There are two extremes to avoid. I have heard players with great ideas who simply did not have the technique to express themselves properly. Also, I have listened to players with great technique who played so cleanly and "legitimately" that they sounded dated and square. In studying the following pages, remember to achieve sharp and clean technique; but keep in mind that in applying technical facility—you must phrase properly so as to convey the feeling and beat of the music. Remember this—Great Technique is an incomparable asset to any style.

Technical studies

It is important to have control and technical facility over the whole range of the saxophone.

These studies will work within the basic written range of: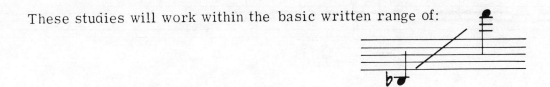

Notes above F, while possible, will not be dealt with in this text.

Movable Patterns
Pattern #1

Notice the "formula" used to build this pattern:
From the starting note, a sequence of half step down-whole step up is used:

A half-step is used to resolve the pattern.

The student should continue this pattern, raising the starting note one-half step each time until reaching:

At this point - go to:

And continue, lowering the starting note one-half step each time until reaching:

And continue, lowering the starting note one-half step each time until reaching:

Rhythmic Variations on Pattern #1

Learning to start each of these patterns on different parts of the beat will be of tremendous help when improvising. Each of the following variations should be practiced using all possible starting notes as described in the previous section.

Movable Pattern #2

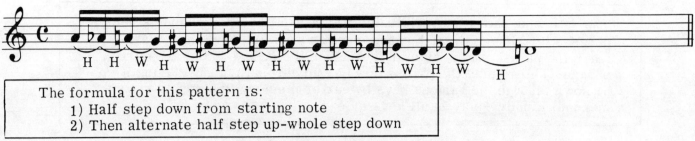

The formula for this pattern is:
1) Half step down from starting note
2) Then alternate half step up-whole step down

Continue the Pattern Up to:

And down to:

Variations on Pattern #2

to be played from all starting notes

#1.

#2.

#3.

Articulation

The following patterns are valuable as articulation studies and as helpful phrases for playing through chord changes when improvising. First-- learn the phrase and be able to "swing" on it. Second--memorize the phrase. Third--play the phrase down or up chromatically (Playing it up or down through the various keys by ear or memory is strongly recommended) Finally--play **in all keys by ear.**

41

Variations on Pattern #1

var 1 — continue up and down chromatically

var 2 — continue

var 3 — continue

var 4 — continue

var 5 — continue

var 6 — continue

var 7 — continue

var 8 — continue

var 9 — continue

Pattern #2

43

Articulation Variations on Pattern #2

var 1 — continue up and down chromatically

var 2 — continue

var 3 — continue

var 4 — continue

var 5 — continue

var 6 — continue

var 7 — continue

var 8 — continue

var 9 — continue

Pattern #3

Articulation Variations on Pattern #3

Chord Scale Studies

In this section, effort should be made to develop both technical and aural (hearing) skills.

Jazz musicians speak of players who have "good ears." This refers to players who have developed their aural skills to the point where they can instantly recognize and react to scales, chords, and intervals which are either played by someone else or that occur in a player's own mind as an "idea."

To help develop these skills, it is recommended that the student play **and sing** all of the exercises in this section. The singing is very important as it will help develop the aural skills internally.

Here is a procedure for practicing in this fashion:

1. Play the exercise until it sounds familiar. **Really listen** to what is being played. Don't ever practice with your "ears closed."

2. Sing the exercise using either syllables, letter names, or scale step numbers.

3. Play it again on the instrument and compare.

The development of these skills is not easy and will probably not come quickly, but serious effort will pay off; and the results are definitely worth the effort.

Chord Studies

The important thing in studying chords is to learn to hear the relationship of invervals within a given chord. Training the ear by applying the following studies will help the Sax player begin to improvise with both technical and harmonic freedom.

Scale Building

Scales are the foundation on which chords are built.
If you can picture a building, think of scales as the foundation on which the building rests; think of chords as the framework which gives the building its structure and strength; and think of improvising as the use of various construction materials, design, landscaping, etc. which gives the building its style. We will begin with the major scale.

Major Scale

A MAJOR SCALE IS A SERIES OF EIGHT NOTES ARRANGED IN A PATTERN OF WHOLE STEPS AND HALF STEPS.

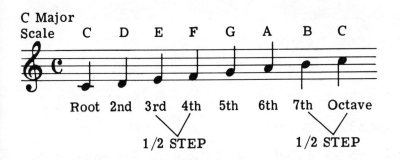

C to D	= Whole Step
D to E	= Whole Step
E to F	= 1/2 Step
F to G	= Whole Step
G to A	= Whole Step
A to B	= Whole Step
B to C	= 1/2 Step

TO CONSTRUCT A MAJOR SCALE WE FIRST START WITH THE NAME OF THE SCALE (Frequently called the Root or Tonic). WITH THE C SCALE THIS WOULD BE THE NOTE "C". THE REST OF THE SCALE WOULD FALL IN LINE AS FOLLOWS:

Scale Tones	Distance From Preceding Note
Root (C)	
2nd (D)	Whole Step
3rd (E)	Whole Step
4th (F)	1/2 Step
5th (G)	Whole Step
6th (A)	Whole Step
7th (B)	Whole Step
Octave (C)	1/2 Step

WITH THE ABOVE FORMULA YOU CAN CONSTRUCT ANY MAJOR SCALE!

G Major Scale

TO CONSTRUCT THE G MAJOR SCALE, START WITH THE NOTE G, CONSTRUCT IT AS FOLLOWS:

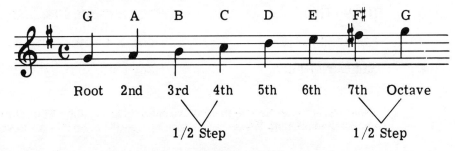

NOTICE THAT IN ORDER TO MAKE OUR FORMULA WORK WITH THE G SCALE WE MUST SHARP (#) THE F. THERE MUST BE A WHOLE STEP BETWEEN THE 6th AND 7th TONES OF THE SCALE. IN ORDER TO ESTABLISH A WHOLE STEP BETWEEN E AND F WE MUST SHARP THE F.

Chord Building Chart*

Chord Type	Scale Degrees Used	Symbols
Major	Root, 3rd, 5th	Maj
Minor	Root, ♭3rd, 5th	mi, −, m
Diminished	Root, ♭3rd, ♭5th, ♭♭7th	dim, °
Augmented	Root, 3rd, ♯5th	+, aug.
Dominant Seventh	Root, 3rd, 5th, ♭7th	dom. 7, 7
Minor Seventh	Root, ♭3rd, 5th, ♭7th	-7, min 7
Major Sixth	Root, 3rd, 5th, 6th	M6, M6, 6
Minor Sixth	Root, ♭3rd, 5th, 6th	mi 6, −6
Seventh #5th	Root, 3rd, ♯5th, ♭7th	7+5, 7♯5
Seventh b5th	Root, 3rd, ♭5th, ♭7th	7−5, 7♭5
Major 7th b3rd	Root, ♭3rd, 5th, maj. 7th	Ma 7−3
Minor 7th b5th	Root, ♭3rd, ♭5th, ♭7th	mi 7−5, −7♭5
Seventh Suspended 4th	Root, 4th, 5th, ♭7th	7 sus 4
Ninth	Root, 3rd, 5th, ♭7th, 9th	9
Minor Ninth	Root, ♭3rd, 5th, ♭7th, 9th	mi 9, −9
Major Ninth	Root, 3rd, 5th, maj. 7th, 9th	Ma9
Ninth Augmented 5th	Root, 3rd, ♯5th, ♭7th, 9th	9+5, 9♯5
Ninth Flatted 5th	Root, 3rd, ♭5th, ♭7th, 9th	9−5, 9♭5
Seventh b9	Root, 3rd, 5th, ♭7th, ♭9th	7−9, 7♭9
Augmented Ninth	Root, 3rd, 5th, ♭7th, ♯9th	9+, 7+9
9/6	Root, 3rd, 5th, 6th, 9th	$\frac{9}{6}$, 6 add 9
Eleventh	Root, 3rd, 5th, ♭7th, 9th, 11th	11
Augmented Eleventh	Root, 3rd, 5th, ♭7th, 9th, ♯11th	11+, 7 aug 11
thirteenth	Root, 3rd, 5th, ♭7th, 9th, 11th, 13th	13
Thirteenth b9	Root, 3rd, 5th, ♭7th, ♭9th, 11th, 13th	13♭9
Thirteenth b9b5	Root, 3rd, ♭5th, ♭7th, ♭9th, 11th, 13th	13♭9♭5
Half Diminished	Root, ♭3rd, ♭5th, ♭7th	ø

*Note—To arrive at scale degrees above one octave (i.e., 9th, 11th, 13th), continue your scale up two octaves and keep numbering. The second scale degree will be the ninth tone as you begin your second octave.

Order of Keys for Practicing

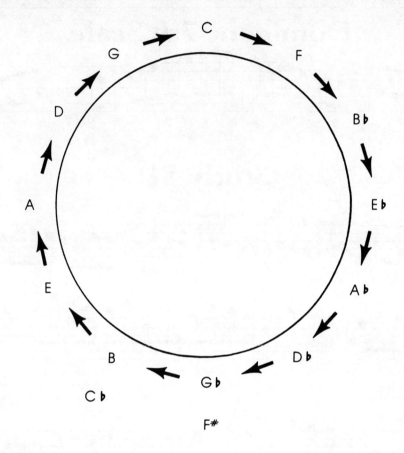

The circle is known as the "Circle of Fifths" because each tone is the interval of a perfect fifth lower than the tone preceding it.

Dominant 7th Chord

* The dominant seventh chord usually resolves to a fourth. (Play the arpeggio and then sing it. Singing is esential for ear training.)

Dominant 7th Scale

Study #1

Study #2

Study #3

All chords, scales and studies should be played in all keys, using the following order and this procedure

    1) Start on the lowest possible root:

Example - in the key of F, start on   not on

    2) Play each as high as possible (up to and including high F) as determined by the notes in the particular chord, scale or study, and down as low as possible.
    3) Play back up to finish on the starting note.

Resolution of Dominant 7th

The dom. 7th usually resolves to a chord down a fifth (or up a fourth).

Thus:

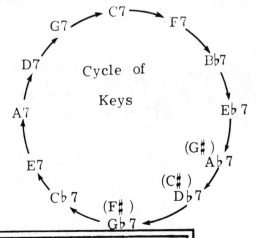

Note: Practice the above studies in all keys!

Blowin' Dom. 7th Through the Keys

Minor 7th Chord

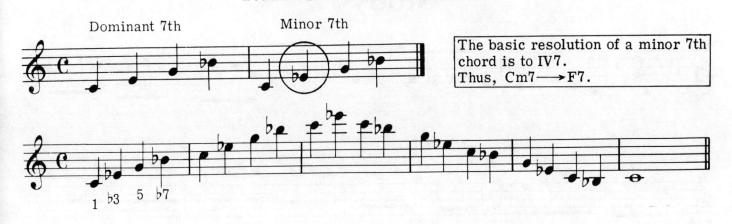

The basic resolution of a minor 7th chord is to IV7.
Thus, Cm7 → F7.

Minor 7th Scale

Study #1

Study #2

Study #3

Blowin' Minor 7th Through the Keys

57

7♭5

Play and sing!

7♭5 Chord

The 7♭5 chord resolves usually in 2 alternate ways.
1. To a 4th step thus: (C7♭5 →) F
2. Or to a half step lower thus: (C7♭5 →) B

7♭5 Scale

Study #1

Study #2

Study #3

Modulating Down 1/2 Step

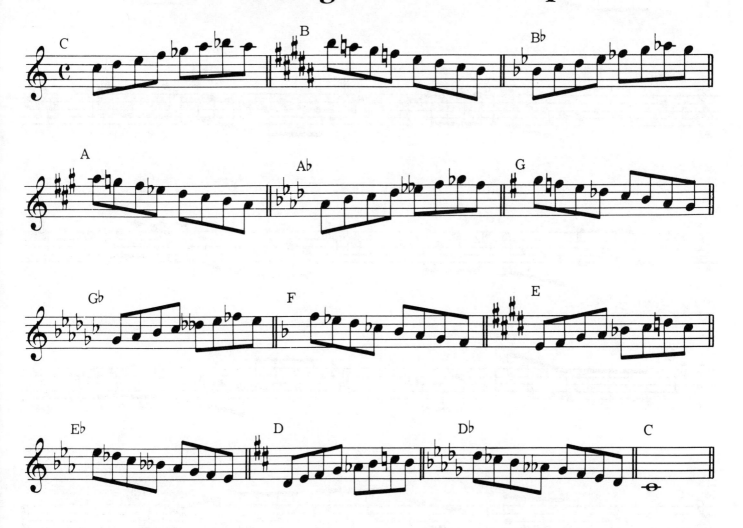

Blowin' 7♭5 Through the Keys

Minor 7♭5

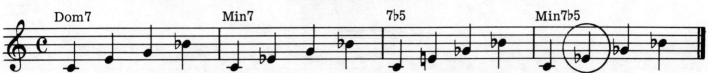

The minor 7♭5 is used frequently when Improvising.
It usually resolves to a dominant 7th chord a 4th above.
Thus: Cmi7♭5 ⟶ F7
Play the following studies in all keys.

Remember-Play and sing in all keys

Minor 7♭5 Scale

Study #1

Study #2

Study #3

Common Phrase Using Minor 7♭5

Blowin' Minor 7♭5 Through the Keys

Augmented 7th

As with most 7th chords, the 7+5 chord resolves to a 4th above.
Thus: C7+5 → F

7+5

7+5 Scale

Study #1

Study #2

Study #3

Changes Using 7+5

Blowin' 7+5 Through the Keys

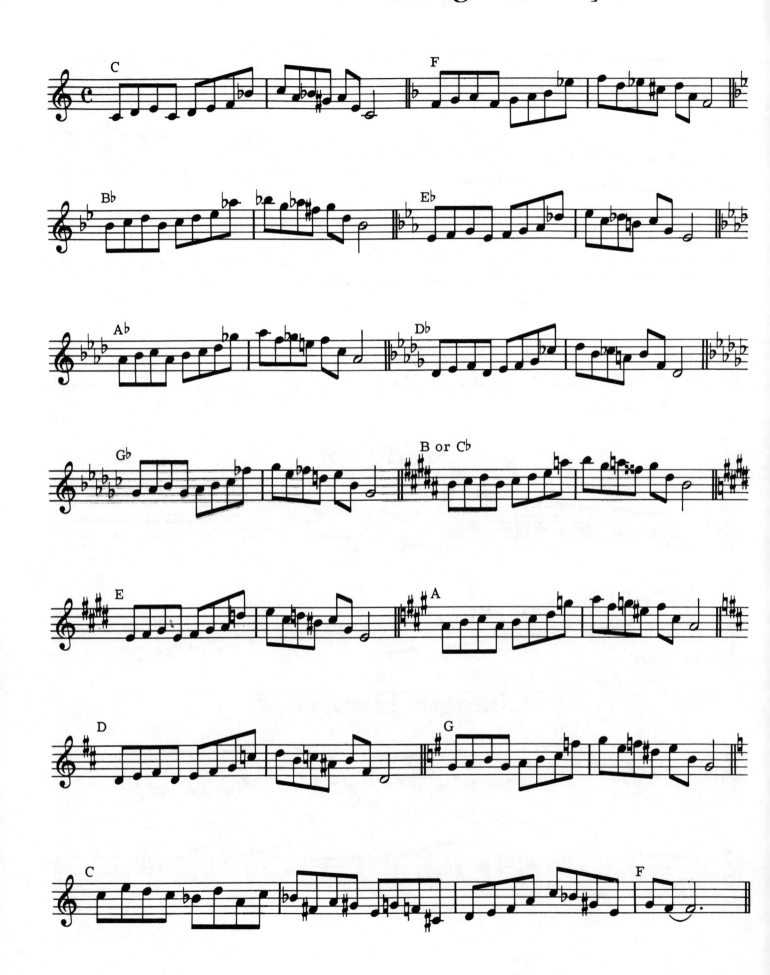

Diminished 7th Chord

(dim 7, C°)

Play and sing!

The diminished 7th chord could be called a minor 6♭5.
A minor 6♭5 tends, because of the ♭5, to resolve to a fourth above.
A diminished chord, however, serves as a passing chord resolving
1/2 step up or down.

Thus: Cdim ——→ C#7
or
Cdim ——→ B7

A diminished chord is constructed by using minor third intervals. In order to create
a scale that will work with the diminished chord, we will construct the scale on a whole
step — half basis.

The diminished chord is constructed using minor third intervals. The scale uses
alternating whole steps and half steps.

Diminished Scale #1

Study #1

Study #1 (Cont.)

Study #2

Study #3

If we begin our diminished scale with a 1/2 step, we have a slightly different sounding scale which will work well when played against chords built on diminished type intervals. (ie 7b9, 7b9#11, 7#9, or 7#9#11, etc.)

Diminished Scale #2

Study #1

69

Study #2

Study #3

70

Vibrato

Vibrato is an important part of saxophone playing. It is recommended that the student listen to both saxophonists **and vocalists** to gain a concept of how and when vibrato is used.

The vibrato is created by a slight movement of the jaw. The syllable "wah" produces a suitable jaw movement. Keep the support and the air stream steady.

The following exercises will help in the development of a smooth and even vibrato. Do not leave an exercise until the vibrato is under control.

Development of vibrato is not an overnight task. It requires daily practice.

Vibrato Studies

4 pulses per measure

6 pulses per measure

8 pulses per measure

10 pulses per measure

12 pulses per measure

16 pulses per measure

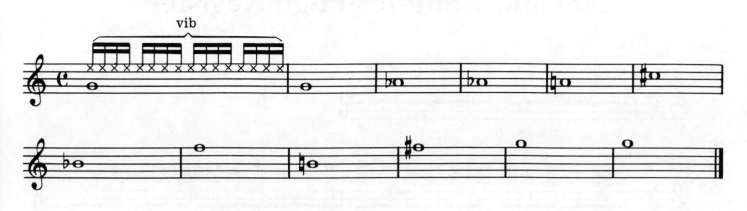

Accelerating Pulse

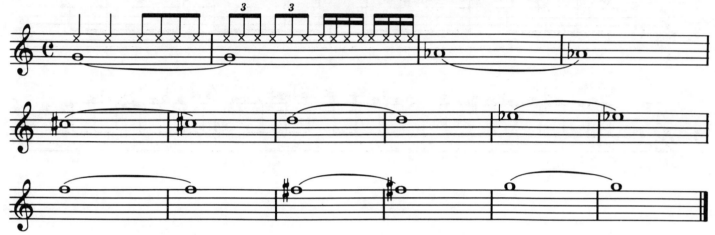

Lush Sounds

Flexibility Studies-High Register

Flexibility Studies-Low Register

SECTION TWO:
Saxophone Improvising

Constructing Major Scales
(See "Building Major Scale", page 49)

Construct the Major Scale for each key and LABEL THE ROOT, 3RD, and 5TH Tones of each scale. Finally, write the Sharps or Flats found in each Key.

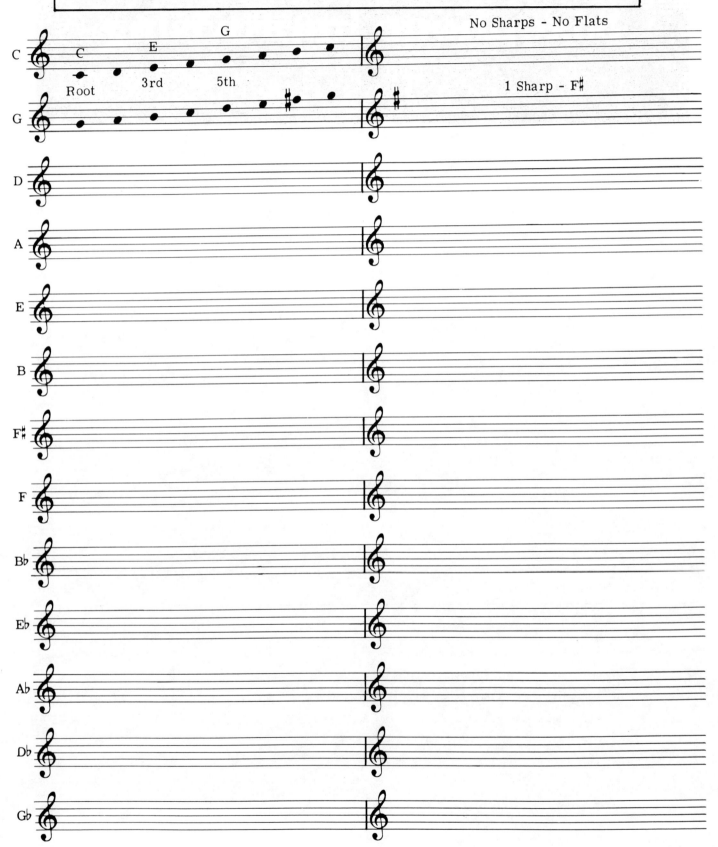

Major Chords

A Major Chord is comprised of the Root, 3rd, and 5th tones of a scale. The notes in the C Major chord would be C-E-G. The notes in the G chord are G-B-D.

Write the Notes of the Major Chords and Label as Follows:

Example:

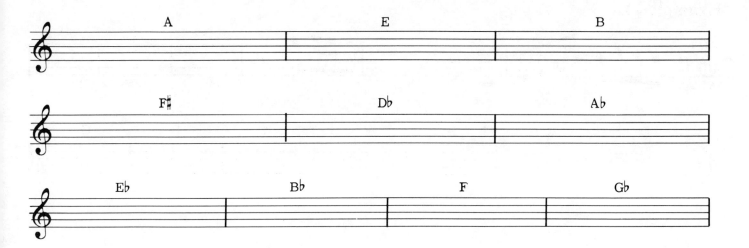

Sing and Play

Sing and play the following major chords. (Sing Root-3rd-5th. Play root on your instrument to check your pitch.)

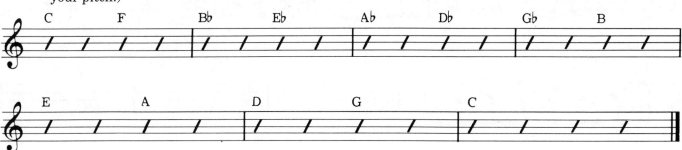

Inversions

Inversions are the different ways in which a chord may be written or played: That is to say, a "C" chord may be constructed:

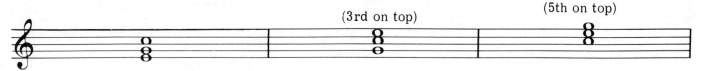

5

Melodic Development on Major Chords

In order to really learn to hear chords, it is valuable to experiment with short melodic phrases built on the corresponding scales. Below are several examples. Play and sing them through the various keys. Next, Invent your own. Write them down and play and sing them through the keys like the following example.

Example #1

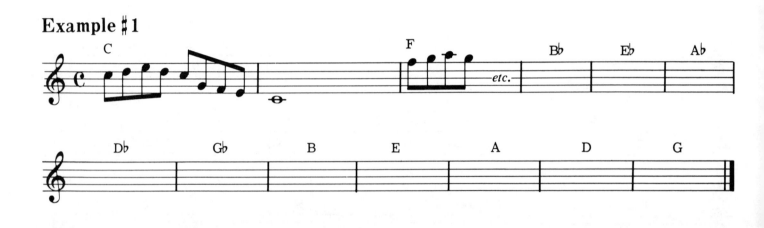

Example #2

Write Your Own

Write, Sing, and Play
(See Chord Building Chart, page 50)

Write and Sing
the following chords

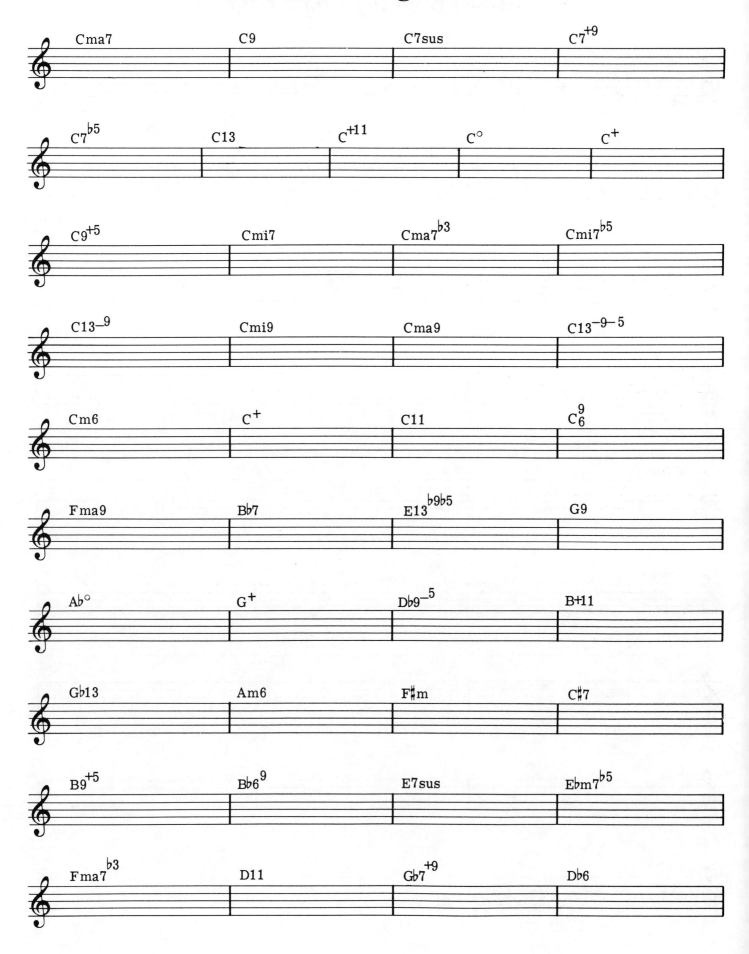

Scale Relationships

In order to understand, analyze and play chord progressions, you need to learn what chords are built on the various scale degrees of a given key.

Scale Degrees
(Key of C)

Thus, the IIm chord in the key of C would be Dm. The V^7 chord in the key of G would be D^7. The IIIm^7 chord in the key of D would be F♯m^7.

Write the answers to the following questions

and spell out the appropriate chords.

1. The IMa^7 chord in the key of D♭ is _____.
2. VIm^7 in key of A is _____.
3. V^9 in key of G is _____.
4. IIIm^7 in key of C is _____.
5. Vm^7 in key of D is _____.
6. VIm^7 in key of B is _____.
7. IVm^9 in key of B is _____.
8. IV$^{7\text{-}5}$ in key of G is _____.
9. IM^7 in key of F# is _____.
10. IVMa^7 in key of F is _____.
11. IImi^7 in key of A is _____.
12. VII$^\circ$ in key of C is _____.
13. ♭Vm^7 in key of G is _____.
14. ♭IIIm^7 in key of E is _____.
15. IVMa^9 in key of A is _____.
16. V^7 add 6 in key of E is _____.
17. II^{11} in key of G is _____.
18. VIm^7 in key of F is _____.
19. ♭IVm^7 in key of C is _____.
20. V^{7+5} in key of E is _____.
21. IIIm in key of A is _____.
22. ♭IIIm in key of G is _____.
23. II^7 in key of D is _____.
24. II^6 in key of B is _____.
25. IVm^6 in key of D is _____.
26. IIma^7 in key of B is _____.
27. Vmi^7 in key of E is _____.
28. VImi^7 in key of A is _____.
29. IIImi^7 in key of E is _____.

Beginning Progressions

While many approaches exist for teaching improvisation, I feel it is most beneficial to:

1. Study chord construction.
2. Study chord resolution.
3. Study chord substitution.
4. Study alternate scales to be used against chords.

Cycle of Fifths

The basic movement of chords in our western music is according to the cycle of fifths. Study the chart below. It could be called the Cycle of Fourths because each chord resolves to a chord built on a 4th scale degree. Thus, C leads to F; or (to put it another way) C is the V chord of F.

Cycle of Fifths

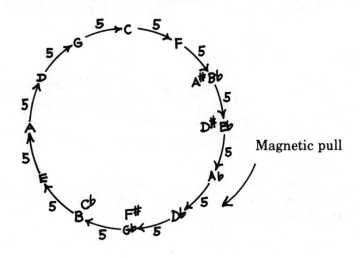

Magnetic pull

Exercise

C leads to _____ (F)	D leads to _____
B♭ leads to _____	G leads to _____
A♭ leads to _____	G♭ leads to _____
E leads to _____	F leads to _____
A leads to _____	B leads to _____
D♭ leads to _____	E♭ leads to _____

83

Dominate 7th Chord

Remember:
    The dominant 7th chord resolves to a fourth step above. Thus:
    C7 ➝ F   G7 ➝ C   etc.

V7 to I7

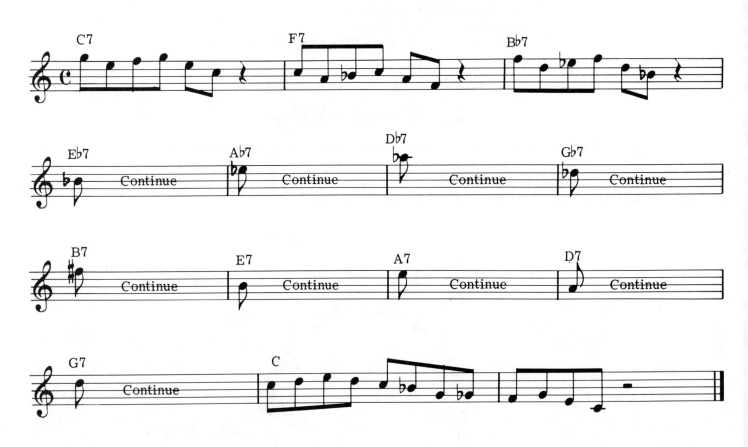

The above pattern started on the 5th of the V7 chord. Write your own pattern starting on the 3rd, then starting on the root, then starting on the 7th.

Your Pattern Starting on the 3rd

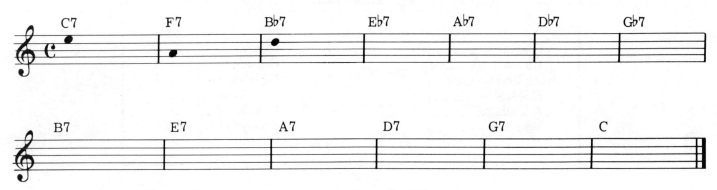

Now write and play patterns starting on root, then the 7th.

Blues Scale

The blues scale works well against major, minor, or 7th chords. The formula for building blues scales is:

Root - ♭3rd, whole step, 1/2 step, 1/2 step, ♭3rd interval, whole step.　　　　or
Root - ♭3rd, 4th, ♭5th, ♮5th, ♭7th, root
C - E♭, F, G♭, G, B♭, C

Play in the following keys:

Blues Modulation

Melodic Ideas - Blues Scale

You should be keeping a note book of your own ideas on phrases to be used against certain chords. Also, you should now begin to try and play solos you hear and like off of records. This is great ear training and will really help both your ear and style.

Play the following ideas in all keys. Then, as usual, write some of your own. The more you write and play, the greater will be your progress.

Play the following studies by ear through the cycle of keys.

Play in all studies in F, Bb, Eb, Ab, Db, Gb, B, E, A, D, G.

V7 to I using the Blues Scale

The blues scale can be played against the dominant or minor seventh type chords. The use of the blues scale in such situations is governed by style and taste. Play the following examples and write your own ideas.

Continue by ear in Eb7 → Ab, Ab7 → Db, Db7 → Gb, Gb(F#)7 → B, B7 → E, E7 → A, A7 → D, D7 → G.

Write the studies in all keys if you have trouble at this stage playing them by ear.

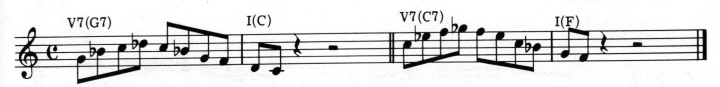

Continue the above study by ear in F7 → Bb, Bb7 → Eb, Eb7 → Ab, Ab7 → Db, Db7 → Gb, Gb(F#)7 → B, B7 → E, E7 → A, A7 → D, D7 → G.

Write Your Own

Write your own studies on V7 to I using the blues scale.
Play each study by ear in all keys!

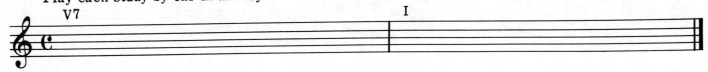

Expanding Our Basic V7-I Progression
II7-V7-I

Play all of the following examples by ear through the cycle of keys!

Play above in keys of F, B♭, E♭, A♭, D♭, G♭, B, E, A, D, G, C.

Rock feeling

Playing Arpeggios

A good way to learn to hear a new progression is to simply play the chords in arpeggio form. Try the following.

Play all of the above exercises and make up your own in all keys.

VI7-II7-V7-I

Play the following in F, B♭, E♭, A♭, D♭, G♭, B, E, A, D, &G.

Write Your Own

On all progressions covered in this text, the more you write, the better will be your playing!

Review Study

Write the correct chord or progressions.

1. IV in key of C
2. V^7 in key of A♭
3. I in key of F#
4. VI^7—II^7 in B♭
5. II^7—V^7 in D♭
6. IV—V^7 in E♭
7. V^7 in F
8. II^7—V^7 in G
9. IIIm in A
10. VII^7 in E
11. III^7—VI^7 in D♭
12. VIm—IIm—V^7 in B
13. $IIIm^7$—VI^7—II^7—V^7 in G♭
14. VI^7—♭VI^7—V^7 in C
15. ♭III^7—II^7—♭II^7 in E♭
16. $IIImi^7$—VI^7—II^7—V^7 in A
17. VIm—IIm—V^7 in F
18. IVm^7—$IIIm^7$—♭$IIIm^7$—IIm—V^7 in A♭
19. VII^7—III^7—VI^7——II^7—V^7—I in D
20. III^7—II^7—♭III^7—♭II^7—I in G

I-III7-VI7-II7-V7-I

Play the above studies in: F, B♭, E♭, A♭, D♭, G♭, C♭, E, A, D, G.

Write Your Own
(The More-The Better! Play Them in all Keys by Ear!)

Write Another

91

Minor Chords

Many different minor scales exist. All may be used with varying degrees of effectiveness against chords in the minor family. We will deal here with the ascending melodic minor scale and the dorian mode.

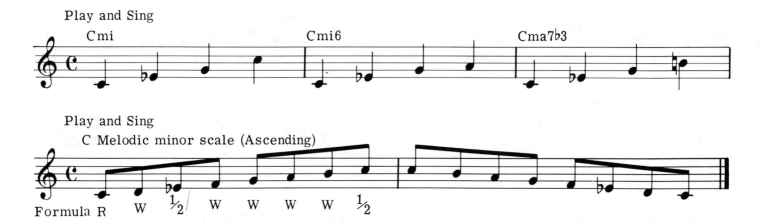

Assignment

1. Play the following studies.
2. Play them again by ear but this time transpose them up 1/2 step.
   Keep doing this until you have played the studies by ear in all keys. (Example-The following study uses C melodic minor. Next, fake the same study in Db minor next D minor, etc.)
3. Write your own studies using the melodic minor scale and fake them by ear in all keys by moving either up or down chromatically.

Melodic Minor Study

Play by ear in Fm, Bbm, Ebm, Abm, Dbm, Gbm, Bm, Em, Am, Dm, Gm.

Simple Progression

Play in all keys.

Melodic Development on Melodic Minor

> You need to experiment with the melodic minor scale. Below are several ideas. Play them by ear in all keys. Keep a note book of your own ideas and learn them in all keys. Alter the rhythms to give your ideas variety.

Play also in Am, Em, Bm, G♭m, D♭m, A♭m, E♭m, B♭m, Fm, Cm, Gm.

Dorian Mode

Play and Sing
Cmi7

Cmi9

> The dorian mode is scale which follows the minor 7th chord very closely.
> To construct the notes of the dorian mode, count down 2 half steps. Whatever sharps or flats appear in the major scale built on this tone will be used to construct our dorian mode.

Constructing A Dorian Mode

C Major Scale

By counting down 2 half steps we get B♭. Therefore, we will now play the C major scale with B♭ and E♭ (The accidentals in the key of B♭) to have our dorian mode starting on C.

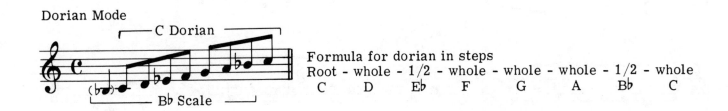

Dorian Mode

C Dorian

B♭ Scale

Formula for dorian in steps
Root - whole - 1/2 - whole - whole - whole - 1/2 - whole

| C | D | E♭ | F | G | A | B♭ | C |

Write the following Dorian Modes

Cmi7   Fmi7   B♭m7

E♭m7   A♭m7   D♭m7

G♭m7   Bm7   Em7

Am7   Dm7   Gm7

Melodic Development on Dorian Mode

Here are some ideas using the dorian mode.
Play them in all keys and write your own ideas. The more you
write, the better will be your progress.

Play in keys of Dm, Gm, Cm, Fm, B♭m, E♭m, A♭m, D♭m, G♭m, Bm, Em, Am.

95

Pure or Natural Minor

The formula for building pure minor scales is as follows.
Find the 6th Tone of a Major Scale and continue through eight letters of that Major Scale. If we take the C Scale for example, we will find that A is the 6th Tone of the C Scale. If we then start with A and continue for eight notes, we will have the A pure Minor Scale.

Example: C Scale   "A" Minor Scale

A is 6th TONE
IN C SCALE

"A" Minor is said to be "Relative" to C. (A is the 6th Tone in the C Scale and the A Minor Scale is built on the scale starting with A.) A table of Major Keys and their Relative Minor Key follows:

The Major and Relative Minor Keys

D is the 6th Tone of the F Scale; G is the 6th Tone of the Bb Scale, etc.

F	Dm	F♯	D♯m
Bb	Gm	B	G♯m
Eb	Cm	E	C♯m
Ab	Fm	A	F♯m
Db	Bbm	D	Bm
Gb	Ebm	G	Em

Finding Relative Minor

To find the relative minor key to any given major key, count down

three half steps. When you begin playing chord progressions,

you will see how frequently the relative minor appears.

Thus, it is important to recognize it.

Relative Minor Key Quiz

1. The Am scale is relative (or built on) the _____ scale. (Answer C)
2. The Dm scale is relative to the _____ scale.
3. The E♭m scale is relative to the _____ scale.
4. The Gm scale is relative to the _____ scale.
5. The C#m scale is relative to the _____ scale.
6. The G#m scale is relative to the _____ scale.
7. The Cm scale is relative to the _____ scale.
8. The Fm scale is relative to the _____ scale.
9. The Em scale is relative to the _____ scale.
10. The F#m scale is relative to the _____ scale.
11. The B♭m scale is relative to the _____ scale.
12. The E♭m scale is relative to the _____ scale.
13. The Bm scale is relative to the _____ scale.

Major to Pure Minor

Write and Play

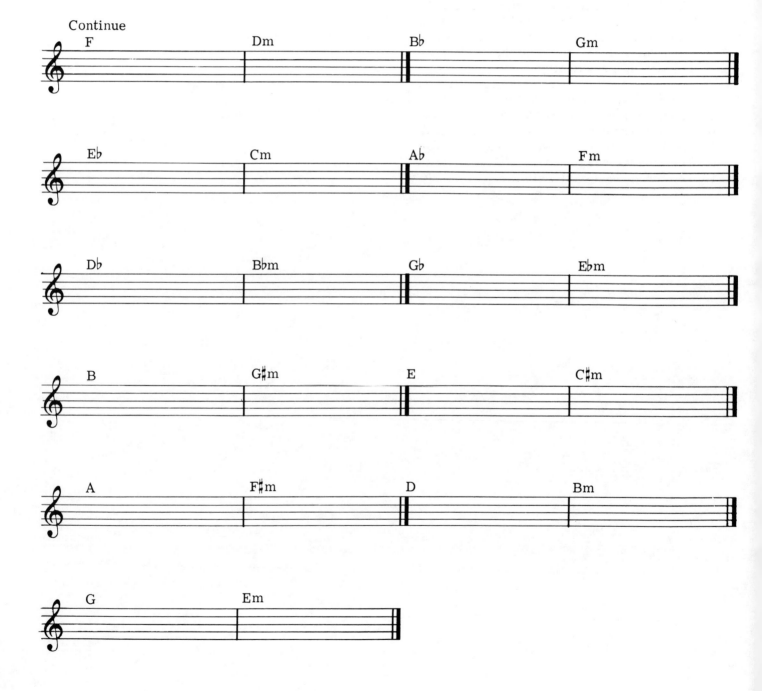

Play the Scale that corresponds to the following Chords

Practice the following study by:
First - Playing the scale which corresponds to the chord
Second - Play each chord for extended periods, improvising
on the appropriate scale tones.

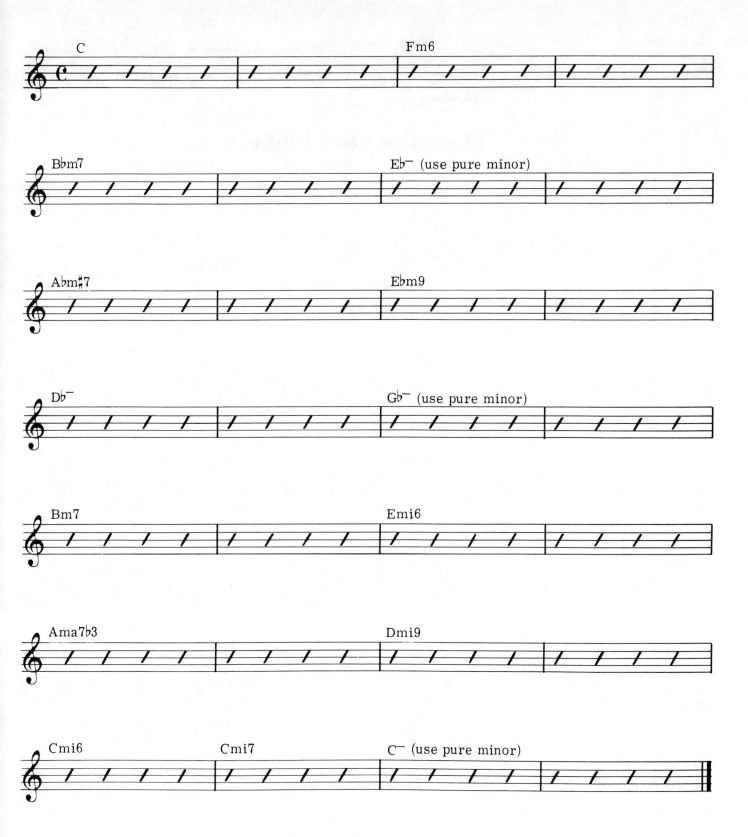

Dorian to Blues

The Blues Scale works well against the dominant or minor 7th chords. In the following example, we will alternate between the dorian and blues scale.

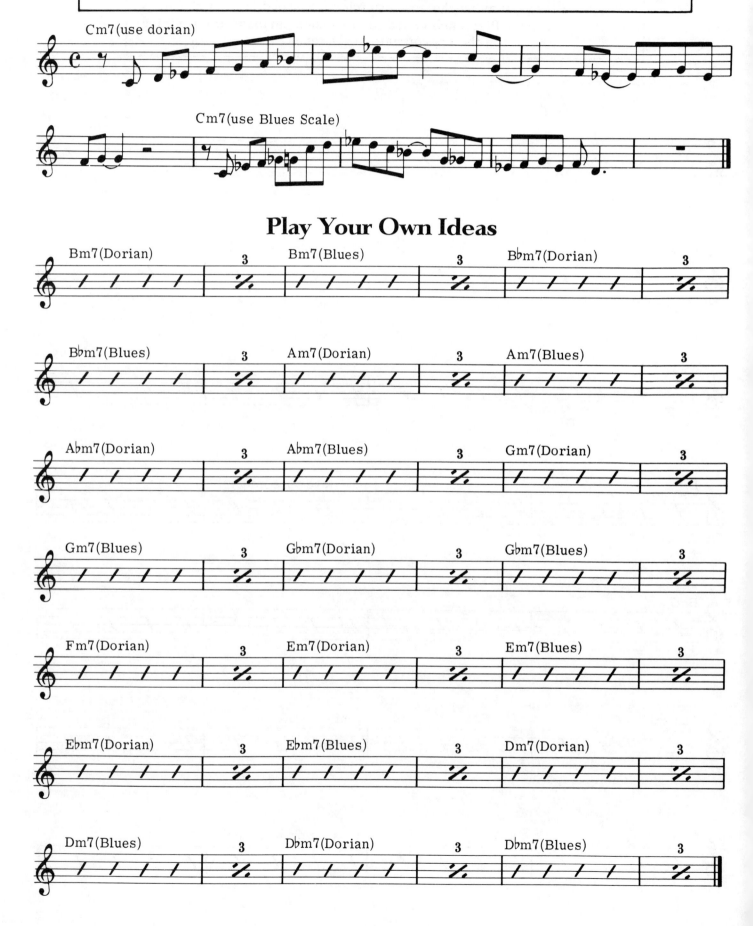

Play Your Own Ideas

Dominant 7th Scale
(Mixolydian Mode)

There are 2 ways that we can think of a Scale which fits a Dominant 7th Chord.
1. We can flat the 7th Tone of a given Major Scale.
                        or
2. We can think in terms of the Mixolydian mode.
To construct a mixolydian mode, count up a 4th and play in that key.
For example: In the key of C, F would be a 4th above C. Therefore, the C mixolydian scale would be a scale from C to C using the accidentals found in the key of F.

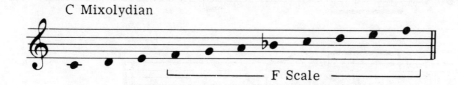

Another Way of Thinking

I find the easiest way of thinking of a scale to use against the dom. 7 chord is to count up a 5th and to play a dorian mode built on that scale tone. Thus:

Thinking this way has the advantage of indirectly forcing you to emphasize the 5th, 7th, 9th, and to some extent, the 11th of the C7 chord.

Play Scales and Scale patterns that correspond to the following chords. Write your ideas.

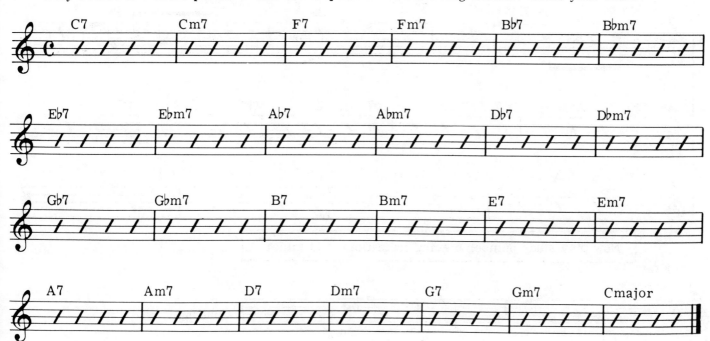

Melodic Studies on Dominant 7th

Once Again, ① Play the following studies by ear in all keys.
② Write your own melodic ideas and play them in all keys.
Remember: A dominant 7th chord resolves up a fourth step.
Thus: C7→F; F7→Bb; A7→D; etc.

Play C7→F; F7→Bb; Bb7→Eb; Eb7→Ab; Ab7→Db; Db7→Gb; Gb7→Cb or (B); B7→E;
E7→A; A7→D; D7→G; G7→C.

Can modulate to relative minor of F (Dm)

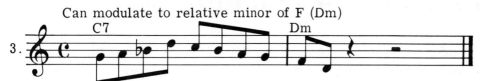

Play Changes

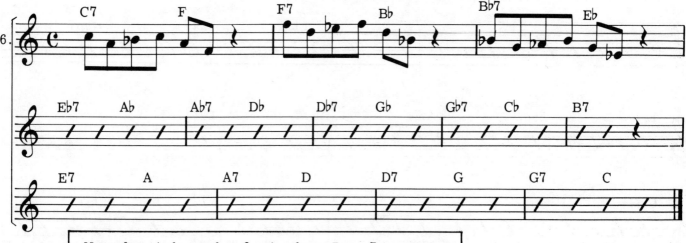

Now play study number 6 going from Dom. 7 to minor

Example

Continue

102

Vmi to I7

The Vmi7 to I7 is a basic progression to jazz and blues. Below are some phrases showing this. Play them by ear in __all keys__. Following this study, write and play your own.

Play above by ear going down chromatically, Gbm7 → B7, Fm7 → Bb7, Em7 → A7, Ebm7 → Ab7, Dm7 → G7, Dbm7 → Gb7, Cm7 → F7, Bm7 → E7, Bbm7 → Eb7, Am7 → D7, Abm7 → Dbm7.

Play your own Vm7 to I7

Another Study

The Half Diminished Scale

The half diminished scale is useful to know because you can frequently use it against a minor 7th chord. Actually a half diminished chord(ϕ) is a minor $7\flat5$. There is an important distinction in how it resolves. When playing a chord progression and a minor $7\flat5$ chord appears, the resolution will be **up a 4th.**   (Cm$7\flat5$ → F or Fm$7\flat5$ → B$\flat$)

If a half diminished chord appears, the resolution is usually to a diminished of the same root tone or to another chord of the same root.(Dma7 → D$^\phi$ → D$^\circ$ or C$^\phi$ → Cma7)

Half Diminished Scale
(Locrian Mode)

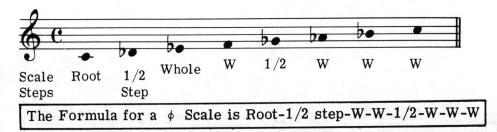

| Scale Steps | Root | 1/2 Step | Whole | W | 1/2 | W | W | W |

The Formula for a ϕ Scale is Root-1/2 step-W-W-1/2-W-W-W

Write and Play the following Scales

105

Minor 7 to ø Study

Play above by ear in B♭m, E♭m, A♭m, D♭m, G♭m, B♭m, Em, Am, Dm, Gm.

Continue in Fm, B♭m, E♭m, A♭m, D♭m, G♭m, Bm, Em, Am, Dm, Gm.

Continue in Fm, B♭m, E♭m, A♭m, D♭m, G♭m, Bm, Em, Am, Dm, Gm.

Continue the above in Fm, B♭m, E♭m, A♭m, D♭m, G♭m, Bm, Em, Am, Dm, Gm.

Continue the above in Fm, B♭m, E♭m, A♭m, D♭m, G♭m, Bm, Em, Am, Dm, Gm.

Write your own study and play in all keys.

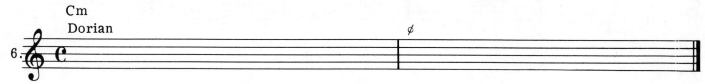

Play your own Vm7 to I7

(Use Half Diminished Scale For the Minor 7 Chords)

Another Study

Diminished 7th Chord
(dim7)

The diminished 7th chord could be called a minor 6♭5.
A minor 6♭5 tends, because of the ♭5, to resolve to a fourth above. A diminished chord, however, serves as a passing chord resolving 1/2 step up or down.

Thus: Cdim. → C♯7

or

Cdim. → B7

Diminished 7th Scale

A diminished chord is constructed by using minor third intervals. In order to create a scale that will work with the diminished chord, we will construct the scale on a whole step-half step basis.

The formula for diminished scale ♯1 is:

Root	whole step	1/2 step	whole step	1/2 step	whole step	1/2 step	whole step	1/2 step
C	D	E♭	F	F♯	G♯	A	B	C

Diminished Scale #1

Study #1

Study #2

108

I-#I°-IIm7-V7

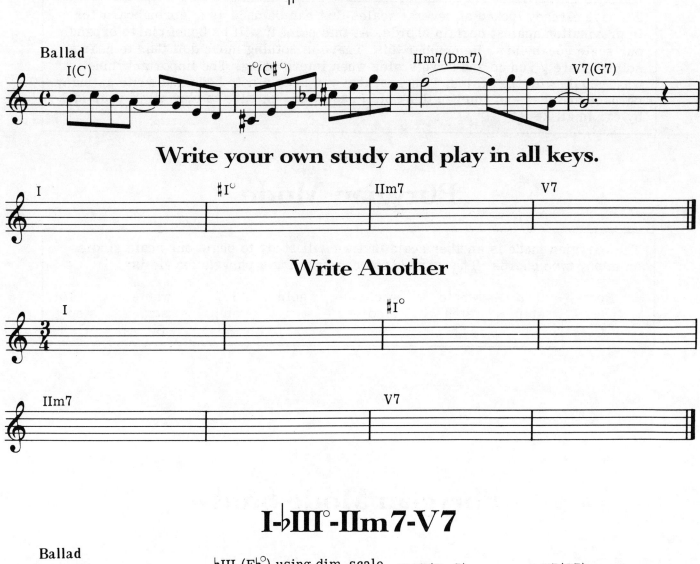

Write your own study and play in all keys.

Write Another

I-♭III°-IIm7-V7

Write your own study and play in all keys.

Write Another

Again

Jazz Scales

We have already looked at several scales that can be used as a springboard for improvisation against certain chords, At this point it will be beneficial to expand our scale vocabulary. Remember this: There is nothing more dull than to hear a soloist merely run up and down scales when improvising. The important thing is what you do with the scales. I suggest that you keep a note book and write as many phrases and ideas as you can think of. In addition be sure to play all of your ideas by ear in all keys!

Phrygian Mode

The phrygian mode is another scale that we will study to begin our scale studies on minor type chords. The formula for constructing a phrygian scale is:

Root	–	1/2 step	–	whole step	–	whole step	–	whole step	–	1/2 step	–	whole step	–	whole step
C		D♭		E♭		F		G		A♭		B♭		C

Phrygian Mode Study

Ear Study

Play the following phrygian scales, both ascending and descending, by ear!

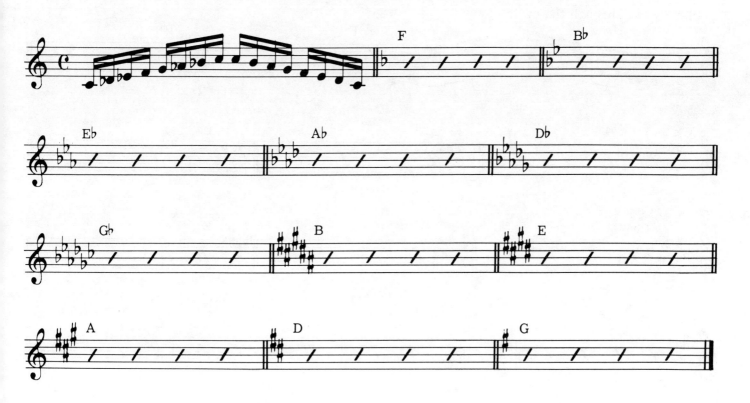

Harmonic Minor

The formula for a harmonic minor scale is:							
Root	whole	1/2	whole	whole	1/2	♭3rd	1/2
	step	step	step	step	step	interval	step
C	D	E♭	F	G	A♭	B♮	C

Harmonic Minor Study

Harmonic Minor Ear Study

Play by ear through the cycle of keys.

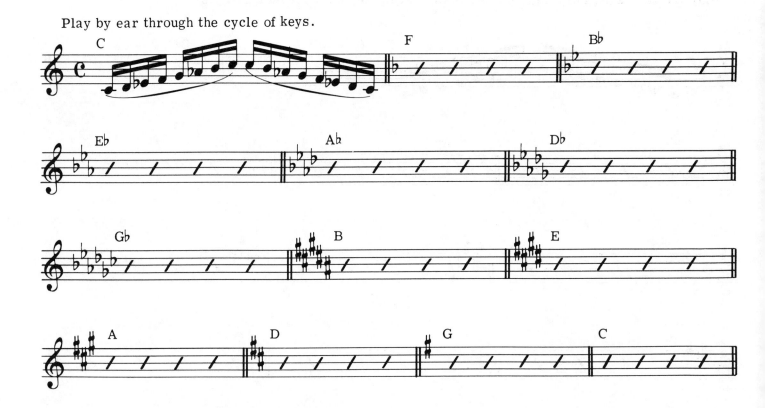

Harmonic to Phrygian

Play by ear through the cycle of keys!
Next, play this study again by ear, only ascend on the phrygian and descend on the harmonic minor.

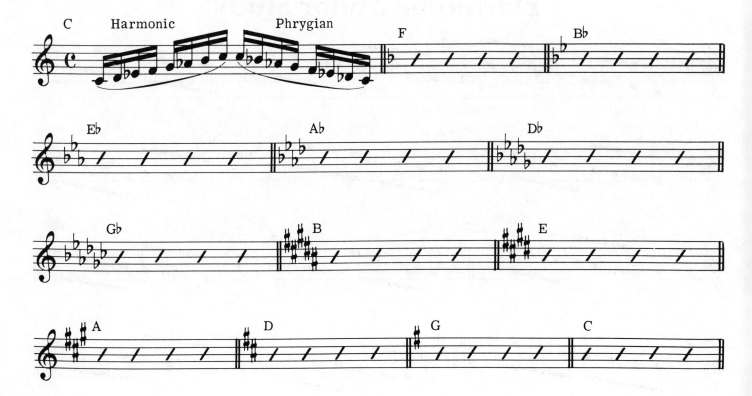

Minor Jazz Scales

Dorian

Formula:
Root - whole - 1/2 - whole - whole - whole - 1/2
     step   step   step   step   step   step

Pure Minor (Aeolian)

Formula: Find relative key-(up minor 3rd)-and begin your scale in that key on the 6th tone of that key. or: R-W-1/2-W-W-1/2-W-W.

Ascending Melodic Minor

Formula:
Root - W - 1/2 - W - W - W - W - 1/2

Harmonic Minor

Formula:
Root - W - 1/2 - W - W -1/2-♭3rd Interval - 1/2

Phrygian

Formula:
Root - 1/2 - W - W - W - 1/2 - W - W

Blues Scale

Formula:
Root - ♭3rd Interval - W - 1/2 - 1/2 - ♭3rd Interval - W

Locrian Scale (Half Diminished)
(Minor Type with ♭5)

Formula:
Root - 1/2 - W - W - 1/2 - W - W - W

Diminished Scale #1
(Begins with Whole Step)

Formula:
Root - W - 1/2 -W - 1/2 - W - 1/2 - W

Several 8, 4 and 2 beat patterns on the minor scales follow.
Play them by ear in all keys. Then, write your own and play them by ear through the keys.

Dorian Studies

1.
Play by ear in Fm, Bbm, Ebm, Abm, Dbm, Gbm, Bm, Em, Am, Dm, Gm.

2.
Play by ear in Fm, Bbm, Ebm, Abm, Dbm, Gbm, Bm, Em, Am, Dm, Gm.

3.
Play by ear in Fm, Bbm, Ebm, Abm, Dbm, Gbm, Bm, Em, Am, Dm, Gm.

4.
Play by ear in Fm, Bbm, Ebm, Abm, Dbm, Gbm, Bm, Em, Am, Dm, Gm.

5.
Play by ear with Bbm7→Ebm7, Abm7→Dbm7, F♯m7→Bm7, Em7→Am7, Dm7→Gm7.

Aeolian Studies

1.
Play by ear in Fm, Bbm, Ebm, Abm, Dbm, Gbm, Bm, Em, Am, Dm, Gm.

2.
Play by ear in Fm, Bbm, Ebm, Abm, Dbm, Gbm, Bm, Em, Am, Dm, Gm,

3.
Play by ear in Fm, Bbm, Ebm, Abm, Dbm, Gbm, Bm, Em, Am, Dm, Gm.

4.
Play by ear in Fm, Bbm, Ebm, Abm, Dbm, Gbm, Bm, Em, Am, Dm, Gm.

5.
Play by ear with Bbm7→Ebm7, Abm7→Dbm7, F♯m7→Bm7, Em7→Am7, Dm7→Gm7.

Ascending Melodic Studies

1. Play by ear in Fm, B♭m, E♭m, A♭m, D♭m, G♭m, Bm, Em, Am, Dm, Gm.

2. Play by ear in Fm, B♭m, E♭m, A♭m, D♭m, G♭m, Bm, Em, Am, Dm, Gm.

3. Play by ear in Fm, B♭m, E♭m, A♭m, D♭m, G♭m, Bm, Em, Am, Dm, Gm.

4. Play by ear in Fm, B♭m, E♭m, A♭m, D♭m, G♭m, Bm, Em, Am, Dm, Gm.

5. Play by ear with B♭m → E♭m, A♭m → D♭m, F♯m → Bm, Em → Am, Dm → Gm.

Harmonic Minor Studies

1. Play by ear in Fm, B♭m, E♭m, A♭m, D♭m, G♭m, Bm, Em, Am, Dm, Gm.

2. Play by ear in Fm, B♭m, E♭m, A♭m, D♭m, G♭m, Bm, Em, Am, Dm, Gm.

3. Play by ear in Fm, B♭m, E♭m, A♭m, D♭m, G♭m, Bm, Em, Am, Dm, Gm.

4. Play by ear in Fm, B♭m, E♭m, A♭m, D♭m, G♭m, Bm, Em, Am, Dm, Gm.

5. Play by ear with B♭m → E♭m, A♭m → D♭m, F♯m → Bm Em → Am, Dm → Gm.

Phrygian Studies

1.

Play by ear in Fm, B♭m, E♭m, A♭m, D♭m, G♭m, Bm, Em, Am, Dm, Gm.

2.

Play by ear in Fm, B♭m, E♭m, A♭m, D♭m, G♭m, Bm, Em, Am, Dm, Gm.

3.

Play by ear in Fm, B♭m, E♭m, A♭m, D♭m, G♭m, Bm, Em, Am, Dm, Gm.

4.

Play by ear in Fm, B♭m, E♭m, A♭m, D♭m, G♭m, Bm, Em, Am, Dm, Gm.

5.

Play by ear with B♭m→E♭m, A♭m→D♭m, F♯m→Bm, Em→Am, Dm→Gm.

Blues Scale Studies

1.

Play by ear in Fm, B♭m, E♭m, A♭m, D♭m, G♭m, Bm, Em, Am, Dm, Gm.

2.

Play by ear in Fm, B♭m, E♭m, A♭m, D♭m, G♭m, Bm, Em, Am, Dm, Gm.

3.

Play by ear in Fm, B♭m, E♭m, A♭m, D♭m, G♭m, Bm, Em, Am, Dm, Gm.

4.

Play by ear in Fm, B♭m, E♭m, A♭m, D♭m, G♭m, Bm, Em, Am, Dm, Gm,

5.

Play by ear with B♭m→E♭m, A♭m→D♭m, F♯m→Bm, Em→Am, Dm→Gm.

Locrian Studies
(Half Diminished)

1.
Play by ear in Fm, Bbm, Ebm, Abm, Dbm, Gbm, Bm, Em, Am, Dm, Gm.

2.
Play by ear in Fm, Bbm, Ebm, Abm, Dbm, Gbm, Bm, Em, Am, Dm, Gm.

3.
Play by ear in Fm, Bbm, Ebm, Abm, Dbm, Gbm, Bm, Em, Am, Dm, Gm.

4.
Play by ear in Fm, Bbm, Ebm, Abm, Dbm, Gbm, Bm, Em, Am, Dm, Gm.

5.
Play by ear with Bbm-5 → Ebm-5, Abm-5 → Dbm-5, F#m-5 → Bm-5, Em-5 → Am-5, Dm-5 → Gm-5.

Diminished #1 Studies

1.
Play by ear in Fm, Bbm, Ebm, Abm, Dbm, Gbm, Bm, Em, Am, Dm, Gm.

2.
Play by ear in Fm, Bbm, Ebm, Abm, Dbm, Gbm, Bm, Em, Am, Dm, Gm.

3.
Play by ear in Fm, Bbm, Ebm, Abm, Dbm, Gbm, Bm, Em, Am, Dm, Gm.

4.
Play by ear in Fm, Bbm, Ebm, Abm, Dbm, Gbm, Bm, Em, Am, Dm, Gm.

5.
Play by ear with Bbm → Ebm, Abm → Dbm, F#m → Bm, Em → Am, Dm → Gm.

Direct Substitution

When major chords appear, you may substitute the following chords. (Your ear should tell you which chords fit well and which ones do not work as well in a given situation)

> For a Major Chord : Use major 7th, major 6th, major 9th, 6th add9.

Write and Play

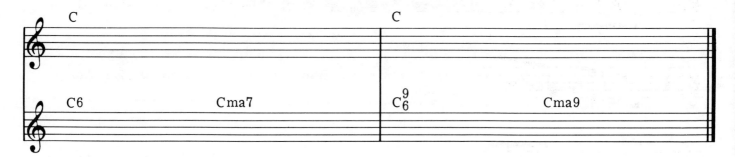

When minor chords appear, you may substitute the following chords. (Your ear should decide   which substitution works best.)

> For a Minor Chord: Use minor 6th, minor 7th, minor 9th, major $7\flat3$, minor 6th add 9.

Write and Play

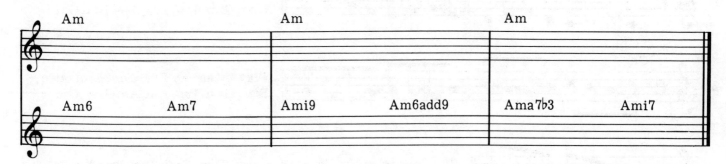

Improvisation Study

(Play Appropriate Scale Ideas with the Following Chords)

Improvisation Study #2

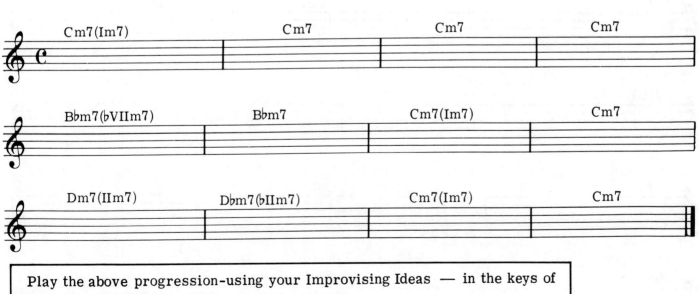

Play the above progression-using your Improvising Ideas — in the keys of
Fm, B♭m, E♭m, A♭m, D♭m, G♭m, Bm, Em, Am, Dm, Gm.

I-VIm-IIm-V7-I

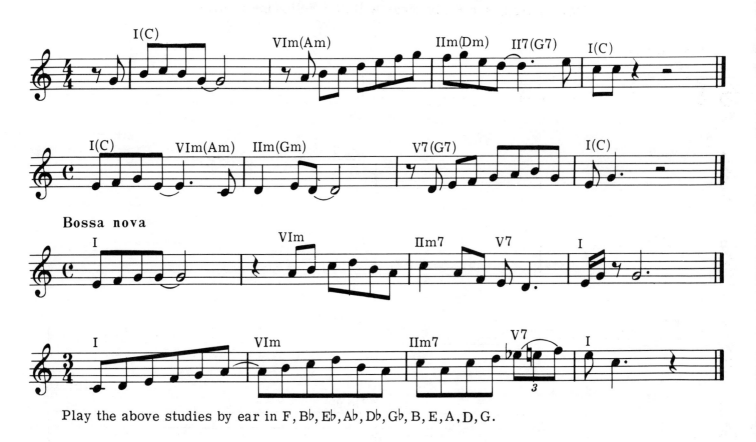

Play the above studies by ear in F, B♭, E♭, A♭, D♭, G♭, B, E, A, D, G.

Write your own study and play in all keys.

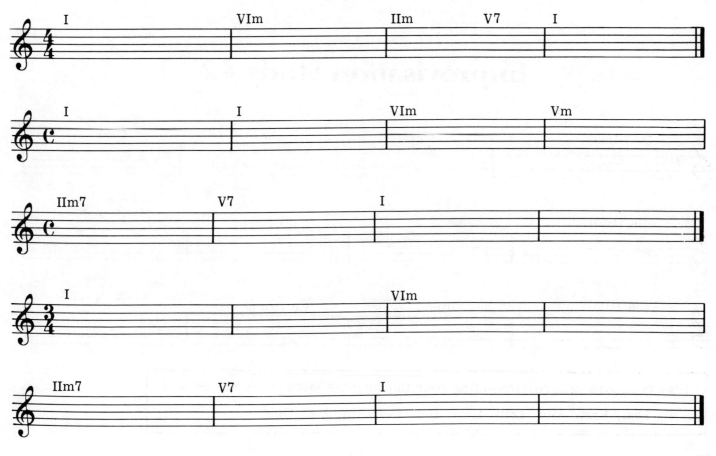

I-IIIm-IIm-V7-I

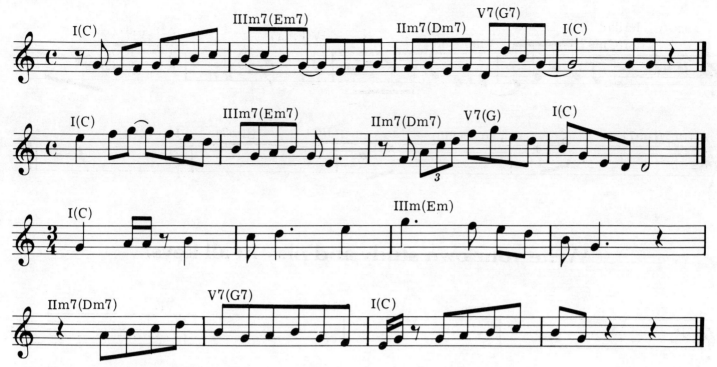

Play the above examples by ear in F, B♭, E♭, A♭, D♭, G♭, B, E, A, D, G.

Write your own examples and play them by ear in all keys.
Remember to use substitute chords as explained on page 34.

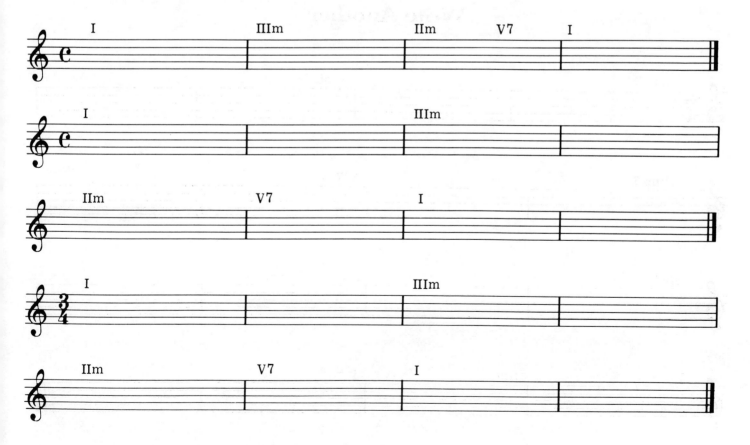

I-Vm6-IV-VI7-IIm7-V7-I

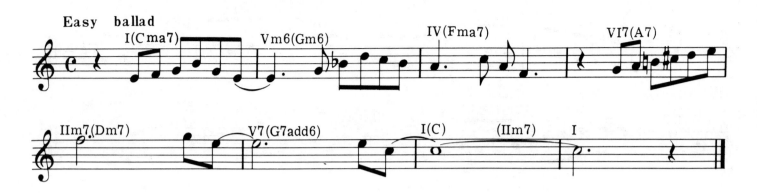

Write your own study and play in all keys.

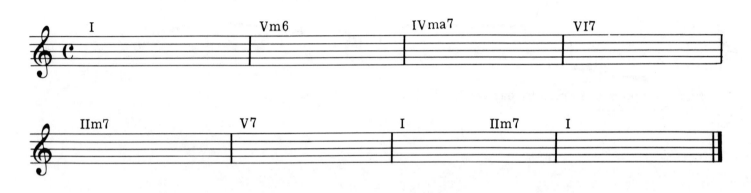

Write Another

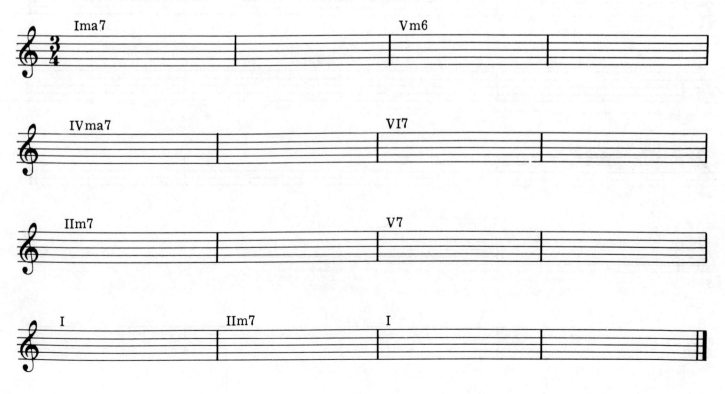

Whole Tone Scale

The whole tone scale may be used against any dominant 7th type of chord with a ♯5 or a ♭5.
The formula for building a whole tone scale is:

Root	whole step	whole step	whole step	whole step	whole step	whole step
C	D	E	F♯	G♯	B♭	C

Write, play, and sing the following whole tone scales.

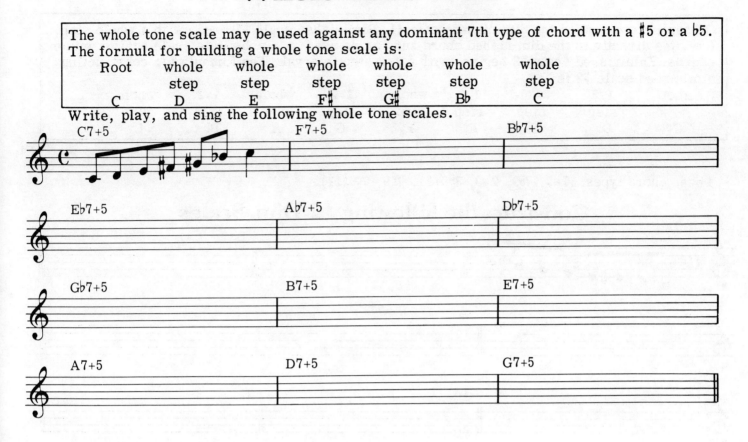

Whole Tone Scales

1. Play by ear in F, B♭, E♭, A♭, D♭, G♭, B, E, A, D, G.

2. Play by ear in F, B♭, E♭, A♭, D♭, G♭, B, E, A, D, G.

3. Play by ear in F, B♭, E♭, A♭, D♭, G♭, B, E, A, D, G.

4. Play by ear in F, B♭, E♭, A♭, D♭, G♭, B, E, A, D, G.

5. Play by ear with B♭+ → E♭+, A♭+ → D♭+, F♯+ → B+, E+ → A+, D+ → G+.

6. Play by ear with B♭+ → E♭+, A♭+ → D♭+, F♯+ → B+, E+ → A+, D+ → G+.

Diminished Scale #2

On page 37 we studied the diminished scale #1. Diminished scale #1 began with a whole step.
1 relates directly to the diminished chord and can be used as a substitute scale against minor
chords. Diminished scale #2 begins with a 1/2 step interval. The formula for constructing
diminished scale #2 is:

Root	1/2 step	whole step	1/2 step	whole step	1/2 step	whole step	1/2 step	whole step
C	Db	Eb	E♮	F#	G	A	Bb	C

These chord types: (7-5, 7b9, 7+9, 7b9+11, 7#9, 7#9#11)

Construct the following #2 Dim. Scales

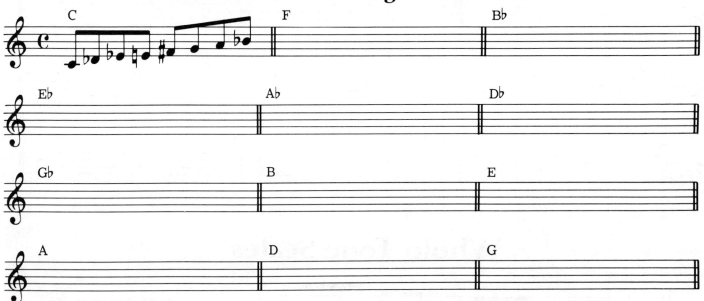

Diminished Scale #2 Studies

1. Play by ear in F, Bb, Eb, Ab, Db, Gb, B, E, A, D, G.

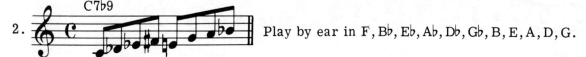

2. C7b9   Play by ear in F, Bb, Eb, Ab, Db, Gb, B, E, A, D, G.

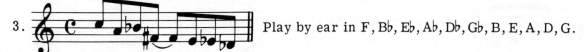

3. C7b9+11   Play by ear in F, Bb, Eb, Ab, Db, Gb, B, E, A, D, G.

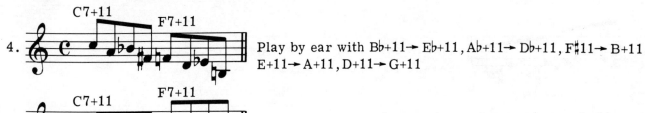

4. C7+11 F7+11   Play by ear with Bb+11→Eb+11, Ab+11→Db+11, F#11→B+11
E+11→A+11, D+11→G+11

5. C7+11 F7+11   Play by ear with Bb+11→Eb+11, Ab+11→Db+11, F#+11→B+11
E+11→A+11, D+11→G+11.

124

Turn Arounds and Endings

At the end of a song, rhythm players frequently add a 2 bar phrase to lead back into the beginning. This is done to relieve the monotony of playing the I chord for several measures. Below are some common turn arounds. Play them in all keys!

Write your own study and play in all keys.

Bridges

The middle section or "B" section of tunes is called "the bridge". Some fairly typical bridges are presented on the following pages. Write solos and experiment by playing them by ear in all keys!

1

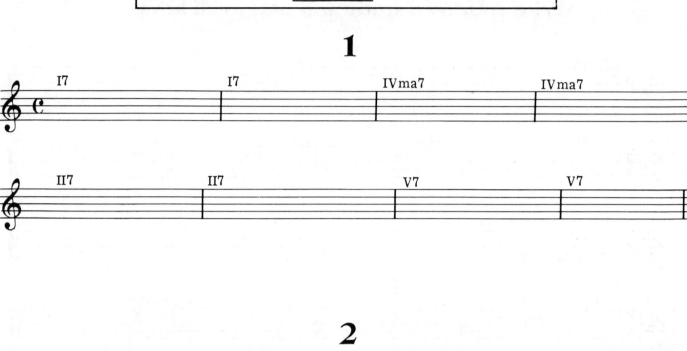

2

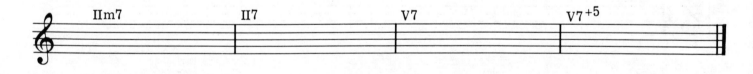

3

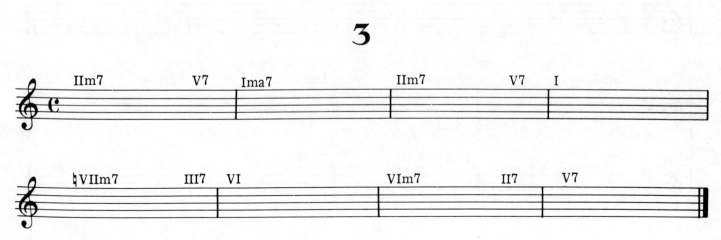

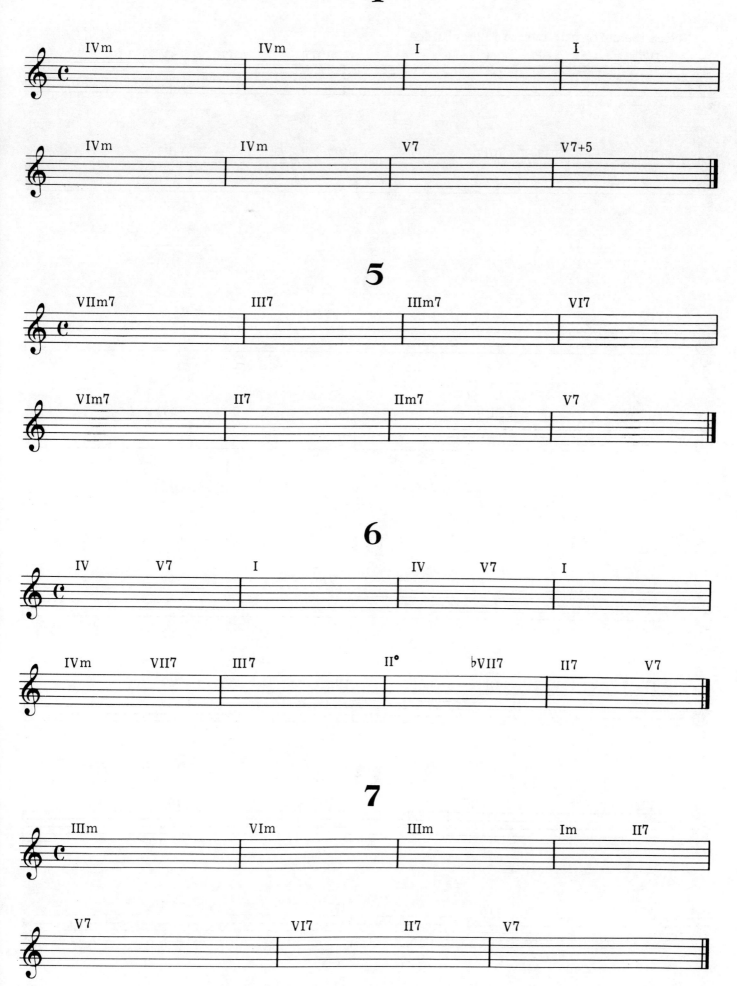

8

Notice the chromatic motion in this bridge.

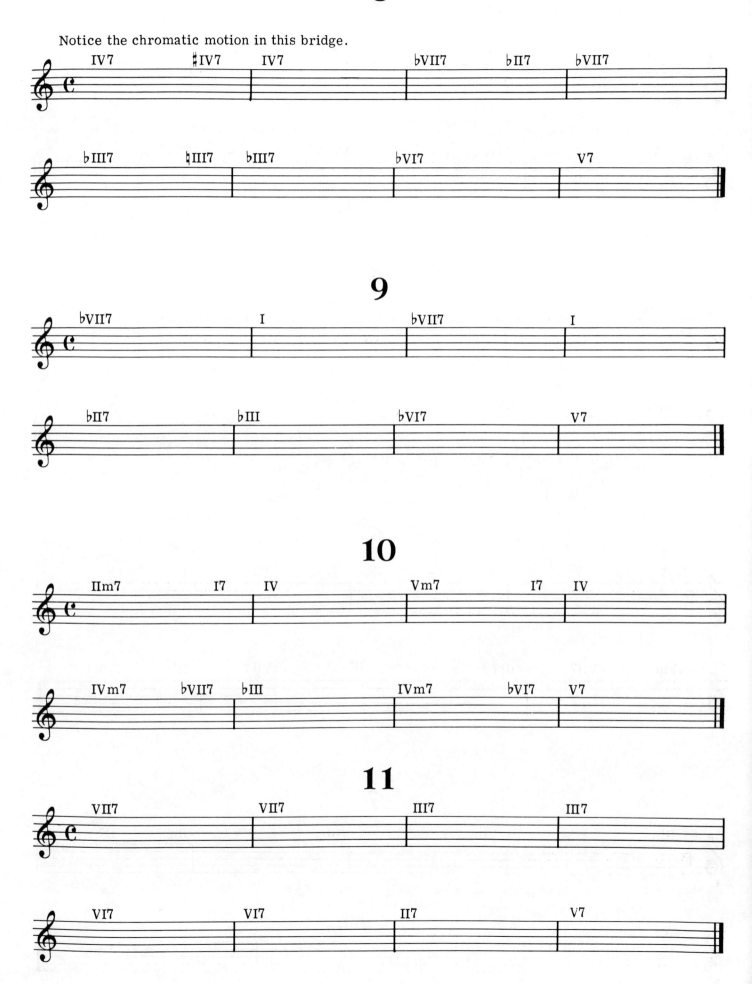

9

10

11

12

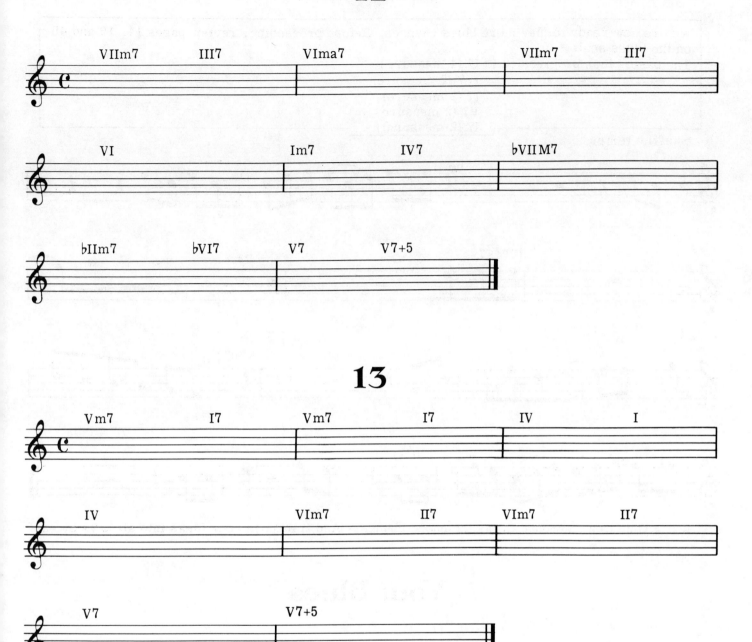

VIIm7	III7	VIma7		VIIm7	III7
VI		Im7	IV7	♭VIIM7	
♭IIm7	♭VI7	V7	V7+5		

13

Vm7	I7	Vm7	I7	IV	I
IV		VIm7	II7	VIm7	II7
V7		V7+5			

14

| ♭IIIm7 | IVdim. | IIm7 | V7 |
| I | VI7 | IIm7 | V7 |

More Blues

We are now ready to play more blues changes. Before proceeding, review pages 14, 15 and 45 on the blues scale.

The basic blues progression is I7 (4 measure)
IV7 (2 measure)
I7 (2 measure)
V7 (2 measure)
I7 (2 measure)

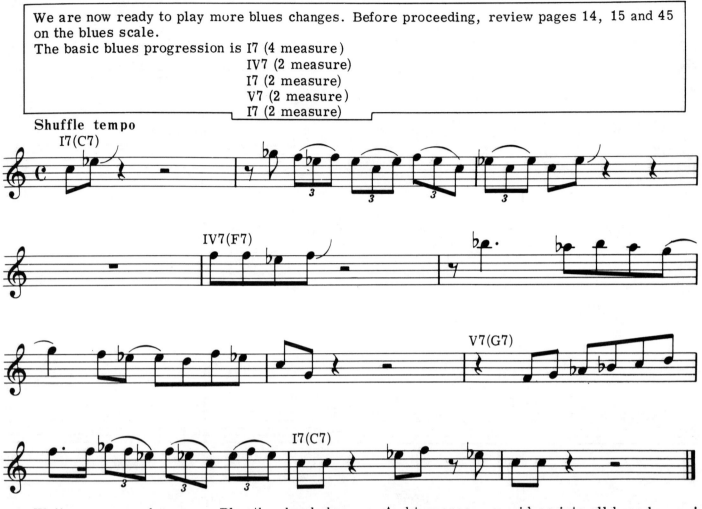

Write your own choruses - Play the chord changes- And transpose your ideas into all keys by ear!

Your Blues

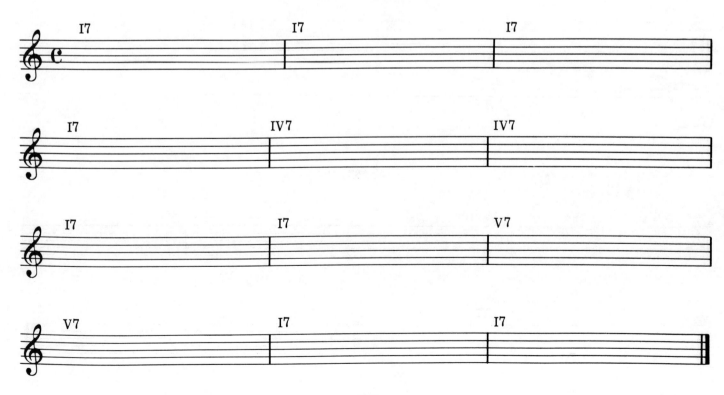

130

Another Blues

Write your own study and play in all keys.

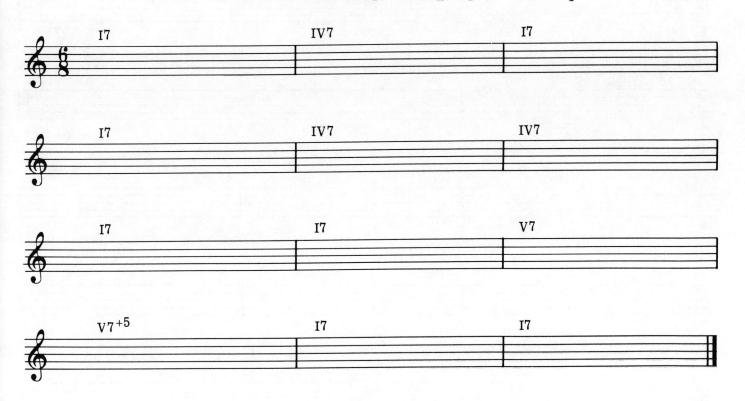

Alternate Blues Changes

Frequently, the basic blues changes are slightly altered. Below are several such typical alterations. Play through the changes, play a chorus or two by ear, write new ideas, and play them by ear in all keys.

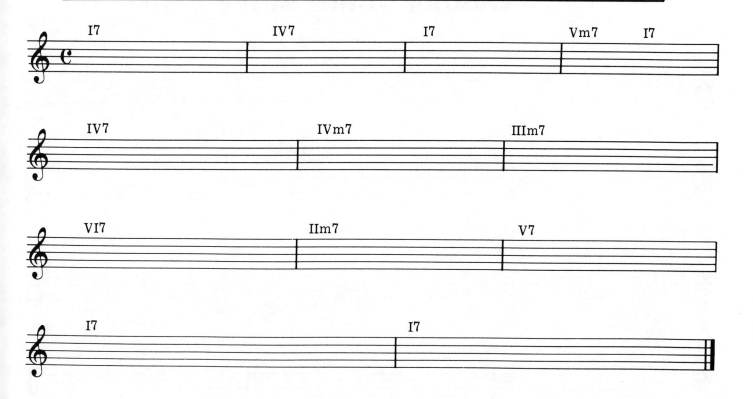

131

Minor Blues

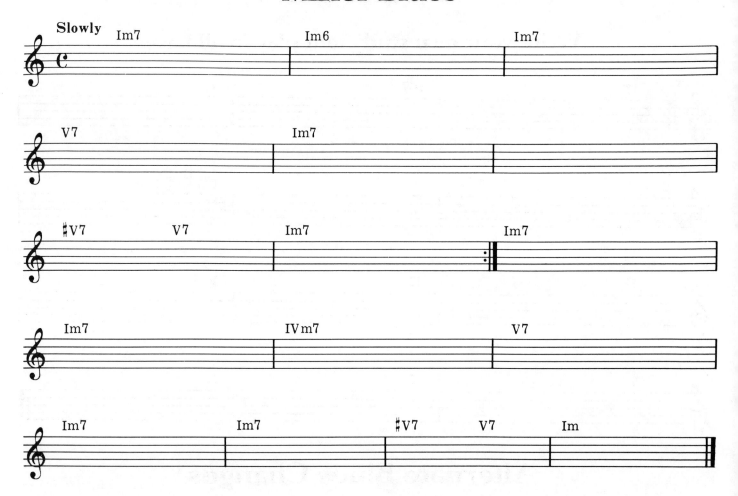

Another Minor Blues

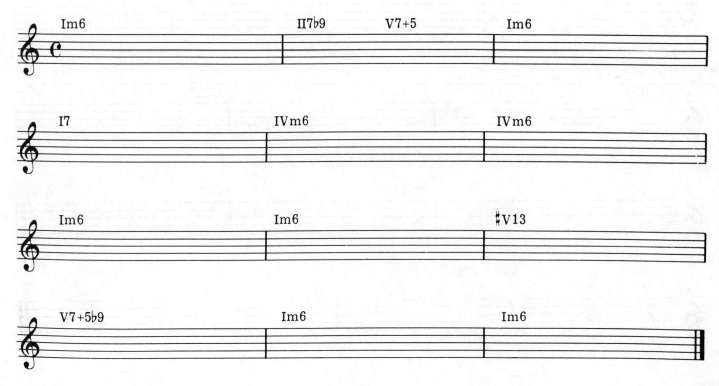

Expanding Improvisational Ideas

We have up to now' been looking at improvisation in a linear fashion.
We can begin to see the expanding range of improvisational posibilities if we look at the various scales harmonized in triads. That is to say, if we build triads (3 note chords) on each note of a scale and use only tones in that scale, we have arrived at other chord possibilities.
We will consider 4 types of triads:

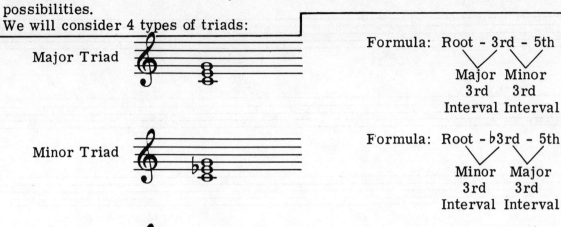

Major Triad	Formula: Root - 3rd - 5th Major 3rd Interval, Minor 3rd Interval
Minor Triad	Formula: Root - ♭3rd - 5th Minor 3rd Interval, Major 3rd Interval
Augmented Triad	Formula: Root - 3rd - ♯5th Major 3rd Interval, Major 3rd Interval
Diminished Triad	Formula: Root - ♭3rd - ♭5th Minor 3rd Interval, Minor 3rd Interval

Major Scale

If we build triads on our major scale, we use this formula and arrive at these chords:

Scale Tones	Chords						
	Imaj	IIm	IIIm	IVmaj	Vmaj	VIm	VII°
Key of C	Cmaj	Dminor	Eminor	Fmaj	Gmaj	Aminor	B°

C Scale Harmonized

To see how knowledge of harmonized scales can increase the possibilities open to you, consider the following.

Harmonizing Major Scales

Using the formula given on the preceeding page for constructing chords on major scale tones, write the following harmonized scales.

Melodic Development
on Harmonized Major Scale

Play the following studies by ear in all keys-Then write your own ideas and play them by ear through the cycle of keys.

Play all studies in C, F, Bb, Eb, Ab, Db, Gb, B, E, A, D, G.

> The importance of playing arpeggios on harmonized scales is that it gives the player a good ear for the intervals within the scale and it gives some ideas on passing tones which create tension and those which release tension.

or - to use a leading tone

Write your own

Dorian Scale Harmonized

The formula for harmonizing the dorian scale is:

Type of triad - Imin - IImin - IIImaj - IVmaj - Vmin - VI°- VIImaj:

    Write the following harmonized scales and experiment by writing and playing your own arpeggio ideas, your ear will govern the use of certain arpeggio patterns in a given chordal situation.

Aeolian or Pure Minor Harmonized

Formula : Im - II° - IIImaj - IVmin - Vmin - VImaj - VIImaj
Write and experiment with the following harmonized scales.

C Pure minor harmonized

Ascending Melodic Minor Harmonized

Formula : Imin. - IImin. - IIIaug. - IVmaj. - Vmaj. - VI° - VII°
Write and experiment with the following scales.

C Melodic Minor (Ascending)

Imin. IImin. IIIaug. IVmaj. Vmaj. VI° VII°

F

B♭

E♭

A♭

D♭

G♭

B

E

A

D

G

Harmonic Minor Scale Harmonized

Formula : Im - II° - IIIaug.- IVmin.- Vmaj.-VImaj. - VII°
Write and experiment with the following scales.

C Harmonic Minor

F

B♭

E♭

A♭

D♭

G♭

B

E

A

D

G

Phrygian Mode Harmonized

Formula : Imin - IImaj - IIImaj - IVmin - V° - VImaj - VIImin
Write and experiment with the following scales.

Half Diminished (Locrian) Harmonized

Formula: I° - IImaj - IIImin - IVmin - Vmaj - VImaj - VIImin
Write and experiment with the following scales.

141

Mixolydian Scale Harmonized

For use against dom.7th chords

Formula : Imaj. - IIm - III° - IVmaj. - Vmin. - VImin. - VIImaj.
Write and experiment with the following scales.